Getting to the Water's Edge
on Whidbey & Camano Islands

© Dan Pedersen

By Sarah Schmidt, Dan Pedersen and Stacey Neumiller

Published by
**Washington State University (WSU) Extension - Island County
Island County Marine Resources Committee
and WSU Beach Watchers - Island County**

Coupeville, Washington

WASHINGTON STATE UNIVERSITY
ISLAND COUNTY EXTENSION

ISBN-13: 978-0-9789853-0-1
ISBN-10: 0-9789853-0-3
Library of Congress Control Number: 2006935686

Recommended citation: Washington State University (WSU) Extension - Island
County, Island County Marine Resources Committee, and WSU Beach Watchers.
2006. Getting to the water's edge on Whidbey & Camano islands. 176 pages.

Refer inquiries to:
Director
WSU Extension - Island County
PO Box 5000
Coupeville, WA 98239
Telephone: 1-360-679-7327

Published 2006.
Printed in Canada on 10% post-consumer recycled stock by Hemlock Printers.

This book was funded in part through a cooperative agreement with the National
Oceanographic and Atmospheric Administration (NOAA), CZM310 Grant Agree-
ments No. G0400250 and G0600066 between the State of Washington Department
of Ecology and Island County, (Northwest Straits: MRC Year 5 and Year 6 Administra-
tion and Action Projects). The views expressed herein are those of Washington State
University (WSU) Extension - Island County, the Island County Marine Resources
Committee, and WSU Beach Watchers, and do not necessarily reflect the views of
NOAA nor any of its sub-agencies.

Additional funding was provided through EPA Grant No. C9-00044904-0 to the
Department of Ecology from the United States Environmental Protection Agency
(EPA). The Department of Ecology allocates and administers funding for this project
(Interagency Agreement No. C0600240 between the State of Washington Department
of Ecology and Washington State University). The contents of this document do not
necessarily reflect the views and policies of either the United States Environmental
Protection Agency or the Department of Ecology, nor does the mention of trade names
or commercial products constitute endorsement or recommendation for their use.

Would you join us in stewardship?

The waters and trails of Whidbey and Camano islands are in our care for a few short years, and then will pass to the next generation and the one after that.

We are stewards, for better or worse, balancing many concerns. We must respect private property, provide public recreational opportunities, protect fragile resources and enable legitimate commercial, industrial and agricultural activities. We believe we can balance them all, and must.

But to do it, we must base more of our day-to-day, personal, voluntary decisions on an understanding and love of these waters. We must think and act more as stewards — for our own generation and the next.

Please join us.

Acknowledgements

This book exists thanks to the vision of Don Meehan, director of WSU Extension - Island County. He dreamed what it could be and worked tirelessly behind the scenes to find funding and open doors.

Many others pooled their knowledge in the effort. We especially thank Mary Jo Adams and Jan Holmes for writing about intertidal life and beach etiquette; Frances Wood for her essays on birds; and Joan Gerteis, Phyllis Kind and Barbara Brock for sharing favorite kayaking routes. We are grateful for photography by Sally Slotterback, Mary Jo Adams, Joan Gerteis, Robert Barnes, Celia Bartram, Bill Blandin, Scott Chase, David Ellifrit, Jan Holmes, Craig Johnson, Phyllis Kind, and Merle Segault. For permission to use maps we thank Green Trails Maps™, Steve Ford of Trax Maps, and Carol Triplett of Friends of Camano Island Parks. Thanks to Harbor Pride for the concept of a Heritage Oak Trail.

Patiently answering our questions were Terri Arnold, Island County Parks; Malcom Bishop, Town of Coupeville; John Crimmons, South Whidbey and Possession Point state parks; Ed Field, Port of South Whidbey; Jack Hartt and Rick Blank, Deception Pass and Dugualla Bay state parks; Rich Melaas, Naval Air Station Whidbey; Hank Nydam, Oak Harbor Parks; Kathleen Parvin, Island County Health; Jan Smith, Island County Sheriff's Office; Aaron Terada, Fort Ebey and Joseph Whidbey state parks; Jeff Wheeler, Camano Island and Cama Beach state parks; Dave Williams, Oak Harbor Marina; and Jill Wood, Island County Public Works Project Manager, 2006 Non-Motorized Trails Plan.

For sharing expertise we thank Susan Berta, Sandy Dubpernell and Howard Garrett, *marine mammals and whale watching*; Steve Ellis, Bob Merrick and Pam Pritzl, *birding*; Tricia Beckner and Sue Murphy, *dog parks*; Melissa Duffy and Lou Labombard, *Coast Salish culture and history*; Karen Prasse and Roger Sherman, *maritime history and photographs*; Matt Nash, *maps*; Doug Kelly and Hugh Shipman, *geology*; Nancy Waddell, *Maxwelton history and natural history*; Donna Keeler, Dyanne Sheldon and Craig Williams, *Glendale Creek restoration*; Eugene Thrasher, *clamming*; and Gil Nyerges and Ken Urstad, *fishing*.

Scott Chase, Dave Baumchen, Alice Blandin, Nicole Luce and Charlie Seablom assisted with site research. Providing valuable consultation and manuscript review were Robert Barnes, Joani Boose, Kim Bredensteiner, Scott Chase, Ian Jefferds, Mary Kehl, Don Ingram, Heather Leahy-Mack, Kathleen Parvin, Rolf Seitle and Arlene Stebbins. Kerry Holland helped index the book.

We gratefully acknowledge those who conceived the original *Getting to the Water's Edge* in 1994. We built on their work: Robert Barnes, Larry Landstrom, Susie Nelson, Don Meehan, Cheryl Bradkin, Joyce Terrell and Doug Dailer.

Contents

SOUTH WHIDBEY

CAMANO ISLAND

CHAPTER ONE

Before You Go
Safety is your responsibility

As you read and use this book, please understand safety is solely your responsibility. We want to help you enjoy the outdoors but cannot assure that these sites, trails, beaches, waterways or activities are safe for all individuals, at all times and in all conditions. This is not a safety handbook. You are responsible to know your limitations, prepare wisely, assess conditions, have the right equipment, understand emergency procedures and avoid unnecessary risks. Users of this book must assume responsibility for any loss, injury or death that might result from the activities described or from using the maps and information presented. All recreation involves hazards. These may include overexertion, equipment failure, changing weather, tides, currents, marine traffic, shellfish poisoning, chemicals in treated lumber, toxic waste or biological matter, obstacles, shifting logs, earth-slide, poor visibility, unsafe footing and falling debris, among others. A sincere effort has been made to minimize errors in the data, maps and other information in this book. **Users must fully accept and assume all risks** from relying upon the information and maps in this book, including any conditions that may change over time, and for any errors that may have gone uncorrected.

Tidelands – the issue of private ownership

When Washington's constitution was adopted in 1889 our state followed the precedent of earlier states and asserted ownership of all beds and shores of navigable waters up to and including the line of ordinary high water (mean high tide). All tidelands in the state thus were publicly owned.

The state made no provision for the owners of upland property to gain access to the saltwater for shipping, to propagate fish or shellfish, nor to engage in any other marine-related industry. To provide access for these activities and generate revenue, the Washington Legislature then authorized the sale of public tidelands to private individuals. Over the years the state sold about 60 percent of public tidelands to private owners before discontinuing this practice in 1967. In Island County, about half of tidelands are privately owned.

'Rights' on private tidelands

We strongly urge the public use **public access** to reach **public tidelands,** and respect private property at all times. That is how the sites in this book were selected. It is illegal to trespass on privately-owned uplands.

Disagreement exists about whether the public may cross **privately-owned** tidelands for the purpose of getting to **publicly-owned** tidelands. The commonly-cited basis for thinking it is OK is The Public Trust Doctrine, a legal principle derived from English Common Law, which is part of U.S. common law but not statutory law.

Under this doctrine, all waters of our state are owned by and available to all citizens equally. This principle affords certain access rights, but is complicated and subject to testing and interpretation in each state's courts. At this time its interpretation under Washington law is simply not clear.

But some things are clear. Private tidelands, uplands and all other private property must be respected. Unlike upland properties, tidelands often have no fencing to mark boundaries. In this book we indicate the length of public tidelands when available, but you won't find any signs marking the property lines unless put there by private-tideland owners. Always obtain permission from private property owners before you remain on, or take anything from, their property. It is illegal to take shellfish from private tidelands without the owner's permission.

To get there legally for sure...

This book identifies dozens of locations where the public may gain legal access to public tidelands. **Tidelands** are the parts of a beach alternately covered and uncovered by the rising and falling tides. **Uplands** are the parts above the high-tide mark, which almost always remain dry but may be partially covered during extremely high tides or storms.

The distinctions are important. Even though the tidelands at a certain location may be publicly owned, the upland parts may be privately owned.

In Island County, almost all the upland parts of beaches are privately owned. Of the tidelands, about half are owned by, and could be used by, the public. The problem is that many stretches of public tidelands cannot be reached directly from land without trespassing on private uplands.

All the public tidelands listed in this publication can be reached by a public road ending at or next to publicly owned upland access. Many of the upland accesses are quite narrow. Tideland users should know that if they leave a public beach access where the tidelands are public, and walk along the beach, sooner or later they will reach private tidelands. These are **not likely** to be marked with a sign. You may not remain on or take anything from private tidelands without the property owner's permission.

For example, a 50-foot-wide public road end may provide access to only 50 feet of public upland and tideland. Or, it may provide access to more than a mile of public tidelands. But in the latter case, except for the upland at the road end, the whole stretch of upland is probably private.

On any beach, the amount of tideland exposed and available for walking or other use will, of course, change as the tides rise and fall during the day. If you walk near the water's edge at any time other than a few hours before or after a high tide, you are probably on the tidelands. However, if you are on a beach at any time near high tide you may well be on the upland. Unless you know differently, you should assume you are on private property.

Uplands – look for the debris line

It's amazing what's right at our feet. Tides often leave a debris line on the beach, and this helps us know when we have left public tidelands and may be trespassing on private upland areas. Generally, most public tidelands begin at Ordinary High Tide, also called the **Mean High Tide.** This is defined as the average of all of the high tides for the last 19 years and can range from 7.1 feet at Neah Bay to 13.5 feet at Olympia. The graphic that follows depicts the various tides. Notice that Mean High Tide is lower than Extreme High Tide.

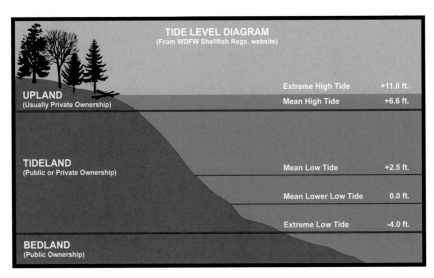

TIDE LEVEL DIAGRAM
(From WDFW Shellfish Regs. website)

Extreme High Tide	+11.0 ft.
Mean High Tide	+6.6 ft.

UPLAND
(Usually Private Ownership)

TIDELAND
(Public or Private Ownership)

Mean Low Tide	+2.5 ft.
Mean Lower Low Tide	0.0 ft.
Extreme Low Tide	-4.0 ft.

BEDLAND
(Public Ownership)

When walking the beach, the Mean High Tide is usually marked by floating debris left high on the beach when the tide recedes. If you have ventured onto the crest of the beach and are walking on the large drift logs that have been there for years, you are almost certainly above the Mean High Tide level and would, in most cases, be trespassing on private uplands.

To complicate matters, upland ownership of many waterfront properties in Island County (those patented prior to statehood) extends to the **meander line.** The meander line is the original surveyed shoreline rather than a constant elevation line, so in this case naturally occurring erosion and accretion make the upland boundary lines subject to constant change. In some places the meander line is now on dry land, but in many cases it may be some distance offshore from the line of Mean High Tide. There is no easy way to locate such a line by examining the beach for debris. *Perhaps the best rule is that if you walk near the water's edge at any time other than within a few hours of the high tide of the day, you are probably not trespassing on uplands. However, it is your responsibility to know where you are.* Please also remember that at high tide, it may simply be impossible to walk on tidelands.

Park with courtesy

When parking at a public beach access, please be considerate. Obey the posted signs explaining the parking rules. They are supported by state, county and city ordinances. If you are caught in violation of these ordinances you will be subject to a traffic fine.

For parking at a beach access where no maintained facilities are in place, follow these rules laid out in state law:

1. No person shall stop, park or leave standing any vehicle upon the roadway. Where no striping is provided and roadway delineation is difficult, no person shall park in such a manner as to leave available less than 10 feet of traveled roadway width. (RCW 46.61.560; RCW 46.90.433)

2. No person shall park:
   + in front of or within five feet of public or private driveways
   + within 15 feet of a fire hydrant
   + within 20 feet of a crosswalk
   + within 30 feet of a stop sign or any similar traffic control device. (RCW 46.61.570)

3. No person shall park a vehicle in such a manner that would unlawfully interfere, obstruct or render dangerous the passage of a street, alley, or highway. Always leave room for large emergency vehicles to have access or turn around. (RCW 9.66.010)

These are some of the more obvious rules of the road, but not the only ones. A good guideline is to be courteous and respect the driving needs of others as well as adjoining property owners.

A few ways to ruin a day at the beach

Every year people underestimate beach hazards and become trapped, killed or injured, or require rescue. Please keep these points in mind:

Tides and bluffs. Be especially cautious when beach walking in high bluff areas. Often these areas offer no accessible upland beach to retreat to when the tide rises. Tides in the Northwest are asymmetrical, meaning the day's two high tides (and two lows) can be of greatly different heights, unlike the East Coast where they are nearly identical. You can become trapped by the incoming tide. To avoid this on a high bluff beach, you must be aware of the daily tides.

Climbing. Please do not climb on fragile bluffs. This can go wrong in all kinds of ways – and does – including falls and landslides.

Shoes. Wear shoes or boots that provide a good grip, and be careful on slippery rocks. The barnacles and other hard-shelled critters found on rocks can be razor sharp.

Hazardous litter. Take some precautions when picking up litter – gloves are a good idea. Do not touch questionable items such as hypodermic needles, dangerous waste or containers of possibly hazardous materials. Note their location and notify the Island County Sheriff or the Island County Health Department.

Shellfish. Before gathering shellfish, recreational harvesters should seek current information about Paralytic Shellfish Poisoning from the Island County Health Department (360-679-7350) or the State PSP Hotline (1-800-562-5632), or go to www.islandcounty.net/health and www.doh.wa.gov for safety updates on shellfish and swimming sites. Shellfish harvesters should always remember to fill their clam-digging holes.

Currents and water temperature. Swimmers should contact the Island County Health Department about safe swimming areas and recognize that tidal changes can create strong rip tides. Also, remember that Puget Sound waters are extremely cold year-round.

Beach fires – what you should know

Any outdoor burning – regardless of the fire's size – requires either a verbal permit or a written permit. Other rules also apply. At times outdoor burning is restricted or banned. To listen to recorded information, ask questions about the fire rules for a particular beach, or apply for a permit, call the county fire warden's outdoor burning information line. You may leave a message for a call back:

- North and central Whidbey: 360-679-7343
- South Whidbey: 360-321-5111, ext. 7343
- Camano Island: 360-629-4522, ext 7343

For verbal permit and burn ban information:
- 1-800-622-4627 ext. 4. Northwest Clean Air Agency.

Please remember:
- No fires near logs or driftwood
- Driftwood may be burned only if you own the tidelands. Call Northwest Clean Air Agency (number above) if you have questions about burning driftwood. Some may be soaked with oil, creosote or toxic preservatives. Inhaling the smoke can be terribly serious.
- No fires within 50 feet of any structure or with winds over 7 mph
- Bucket and shovel required to help put fire out
- No unattended fires
- No fire larger than you can easily extinguish
- Always douse fire completely with water prior to leaving

How we sized up sites

People use tidelands many different ways, so we tried to include what you would like to know. A restroom and drinking water are important to most, but if you're gathering a group you may also need ample parking and picnic tables, barbecue grills and a playground. If trailering a big boat you will need a worthy ramp. But if kayaking, you may only require a gravelly beach on which to hand-carry boats to the water. We point out beach-walking opportunities for sites with 600 or more feet of public tidelands. And if you require wheelchair-accessible facilities, we indicate which sites have them. We include beaches with shellfish resources, together with checklists of safety guidelines and sustainable practices, and indicate sites often used for swimming, shore casting and bird watching. Whether your goal is to enjoy the view from a parked car or explore miles of public shoreline, you will find what you're seeking on these pages.

Phone numbers to keep handy

State agencies: WDFW – Fish & Wildlife. WDOH – Health. WDNR – Natural Resources. Federal: NOAA – Oceanographic and Atmospheric Administration

9-1-1	Emergencies – fire, ambulance, police
360-678-6116	Sheriff Island County – north, central Whidbey
360-321-4400	Sheriff – south Whidbey
360-629-2224	Sheriff – Camano
800-477-6224	Derelict fishing gear, poaching or dangerous wildlife, WDFW
800-853-1964	Enforcement hotline, National Marine Fisheries Service
877-485-7316	Fish consumption advisories, WDOH
866-246-9453	Fishing and hunting license sales, Vehicle Use Permit, WDFW
360-902-2500	Fishing rule change hotline
360-943-7325	Gray whale sightings, Cascadia Research
800-852-1964	Marine mammal harassment, NOAA
360-678-3765	Marine mammal strandings (see pages 31, 77) – Whidbey
360-387-8299	Marine mammal strandings – Camano
800-622-4627	NW Clean Air Agency (beach fires), dial ext. 4
800-258-5990	Oil or chemical spills, Wash. Emergency Management (24 hr)
800-222-4737	Oiled birds, WDFW
866-672-2638	Orca whale sightings, marine mammal strandings, Orca Network
800-732-6985	Poison Information Center (24 hr)
800-562-5632	Shellfish safety (PSP) hotline, WDOH
866-880-5431	Shellfish rule change hotline, licenses, WDFW
800-527-3305	Wildfires and woodcutting, WDNR
425-775-1311	WDFW North Puget Sound office
360-856-3500	WDNR NW Region office

Island County

You may direct-dial any department using its full number. To dial as a local call from outside the Coupeville area, dial the local switchboard for your area and enter the department's four-digit extension. If no extension is given, you may assume it is the last four digits of the department's direct-dial number.

360-678-5111	Switchboard – north and central Whidbey
360-321-5111	Switchboard – south Whidbey
360-629-4522	Switchboard – Camano
360-387-3443	Island County Camano Annex
360-679-7327	WSU Extension or Marine Resources Committee
360-679-7391	Beach Watchers – Whidbey
360-387-3443	Beach Watchers – Camano, ext. 258
360-679-7350	Health – Environmental (shellfish safety)
360-240-5532	Parks
(Switchboard)	Shore Stewards, ext. 6012

MARINE STEWARDSHIP AREAS

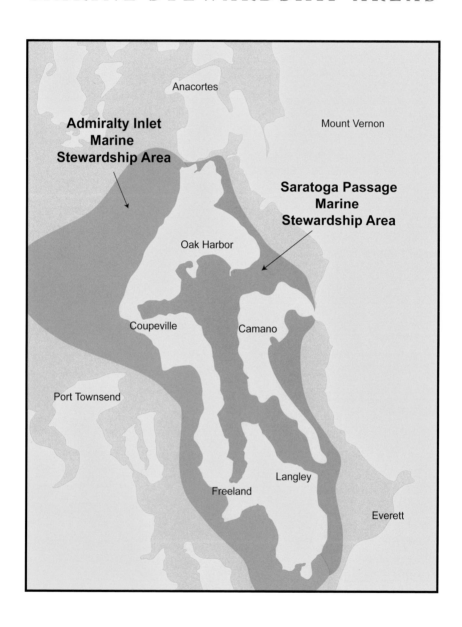

CHAPTER TWO

Stewardship

Why stewardship matters

We depend for our lives on clean water and a healthy environment. For better or worse, we are stewards of the natural world for the next generation. The condition in which we leave it is our legacy. Stewardship is about accepting personal responsibility to learn about, respect and care for that which is in our trust.

How you can help

As you explore and enjoy the waters and woods of Whidbey and Camano islands, please be a good steward of our beaches, trails and marine life. Learn all you can. Observe carefully. Be sure that your actions help, rather than harm, the creatures and environment you leave for your children and grandchildren. Help others understand, as well.

Admiralty Inlet and Saratoga Passage Marine Stewardship Areas

Two large marine stewardship areas encompass all Island County waters. County leaders created these stewardship areas in 2003 to encourage the public to learn all they can about voluntary stewardship and practice it in their day-to-day use of our beaches, waters and uplands.

The future health and productivity of our waters will be determined by millions of individual decisions made by hundreds of thousands of residents and visitors. It is neither possible nor desirable to control all those decisions with laws. Education, public understanding and voluntary behavior change are essential in shaping the legacy our generation will leave for the next.

Saratoga Passage Marine Stewardship Area

On Dec. 22, 2003, Island County Commissioners passed resolution C-126-03 creating the Saratoga Passage Marine Stewardship Area. This designation recognizes the vital importance of Saratoga Passage, Skagit Bay and Port Susan to salmon, forage fish and other marine life. For centuries, the waters between Camano and Whidbey islands have provided a rich and relatively low-energy marine environment of extensive eelgrass beds and small coastal lagoons that afford shelter to juvenile salmon and abundant spawning beaches for forage fish. Three major salmon-producing rivers – the Skagit, Stillaguamish and Snohomish – feed into these waters.

Admiralty Inlet Marine Stewardship Area

The ways in which salmon, trout and other migratory fish and birds use Whidbey Island's western shoreline is the focus of increasing study by the Marine Resources Committee, Beach Watchers and other organizations. This exposed shoreline is one of the highest-energy marine environments in Puget Sound. It not only lies on heavily-trafficked shipping lanes but serves as a major migration corridor for salmon entering and leaving Puget Sound and offers a number of estuaries that provide critical shelter. On Dec. 22, 2003, Island County Commissioners designated these waters the Admiralty Inlet Marine Stewardship Area, calling upon local citizens and visitors to focus increased efforts to understand and care for them.

Become a Beach Watcher

One of the best ways to learn about our shores and marine life is to enroll in Washington State University (WSU) Beach Watchers training. This program was founded in Island County and recently expanded to six other counties of northern Puget Sound. It is a fascinating and deeply satisfying educational program that will enrich your life. Beach Watchers receive more than 100 hours of classroom and field training in a wide range of topics including forestry, coastal geology, marine biology, watersheds, septic systems, beach monitoring, marine estuaries and more. In return, Beach Watchers make a commitment to give back to the community. They share their knowledge by performing at least 100 hours of service in community outreach programs.

For much more information or to enroll in Beach Watchers training, please visit www.beachwatchers.wsu.edu or call 360-679-7391 (north and central Whidbey), 321-5111 ext. 7391 (south Whidbey), or 387-3443 ext. 258 (Camano).

Become a Shore Steward

If you live along the shore, rent shoreline property or belong to a community with shared beach access in Island County you can become a Certified Shore Steward. For information, visit the Shore Stewards website, www.shorestewards.org or call 360-629-4522 ext. 6012 (Camano), 321-5111 ext. 6012 (south Whidbey), or 678-5111, ext. 6012 (central and north Whidbey).

Shore Stewards voluntarily follow 10 wildlife-friendly guidelines in caring for their beaches, bluffs, gardens and homes. These simple but important practices help create and preserve a healthy shoreline environment for fish, wildlife, birds and people. In return, Shore Stewards receive official certification and the *Guide for Shoreline Living*, packed with helpful ideas and tips. The cost? Nothing. No fee to join. No dues. No meetings. No required classes.

The 10 Guidelines for Shoreline Living

+ Use water wisely
+ Maintain your septic system
+ Limit pesticide and fertilizer use
+ Manage upland water runoff
+ Encourage native plants and trees
+ Know permit procedures for shoreline development
+ Develop on bluffs with care
+ Minimize bulkheads, docks and other structures
+ Respect intertidal life
+ Preserve eelgrass beds and forage fish spawning habitat

How and why to join Shore Stewards

Contact the Shore Stewards coordinator by e-mail at shorestewards@wsu. edu, or call any of the phone numbers listed above to receive your application. It's easy to join and your application can be completed by telephone.

Membership brings many benefits, probably none greater than the useful ideas and new information you will get to help care for your property. You will receive a free monthly newsletter, as well as a copy of the resource-packed *Guide for Shoreline Living*, a Shore Stewards window decal, optional Shore Stewards yard sign and a standing invitation to attend Shore Stewards workshops and programs if interested. It all comes with an extra measure of pride and satisfaction, gained from greater understanding and enjoyment of nature and your property.

What you must do to your property

You may do as much or as little as you wish – Shore Stewards is educational and voluntary. No particular changes are required. You are encouraged to learn about the 10 guidelines for shoreline living. The more you understand and apply these guidelines, the more they will help you make your property more attractive and healthy for fish, wildlife and people.

The reasons to certify your property

Owning a beautiful home overlooking a "dead" sea takes something away from the Northwest lifestyle. One of the biggest reasons people move here is to enjoy the salmon and birds, shellfish and whales, and all the other wildlife and marine life of our natural setting. It makes sense on many levels to certify your property. Some people do it for their children and grandchildren, as part of a personal commitment to leave healthier, more abundant shorelines to those who will follow. Others do it to make a difference – to benefit all lifeforms in the diverse marine wildlife habitat. People become Shore Stewards to get to know others who share their passion for our natural setting or to find experts who can help them make the best decisions for the long-term health of their property and shoreline. They do it to enhance the value of their investment, since the program offers advice and recommendations that may result in higher property values.

The Marine Resources Committees

Since 1999, efforts to understand and protect the diversity of life in our nearshore waters have been led by citizen-based Marine Resources Committees (MRCs) in all seven counties of northern Puget Sound. These committees report to their local county commissioners and to the Northwest Straits Commission, which was established under federal legislation co-sponsored by U.S. Senator Patty Murray and Congressman Jack Metcalf. Island County MRC brings together scientists, business people, farmers, educators, recreational boaters, sport anglers, lawyers, county employees, port commissioners and Navy interests in this shared effort. Aided by dedicated WSU Beach Watcher volunteers, the Island County MRC has mapped, photographed and videotaped every foot of Island County's 212 miles of shoreline. They have compiled the most comprehensive database ever created of critical eelgrass beds, forage fish spawning beaches, shoreline hardening features and feeder bluffs. They work in close cooperation with the Island County Salmon Recovery Program to protect and restore nearshore habitats, and with other county committees and departments concerned about water quality, such as the Water Resources Advisory Committee (WRAC) and Salmon Technical Advisory Group (Salmon TAG). More information about Island County MRC may be found at www.islandcountymrc.org. To learn more about the Northwest Straits Commission, visit www.nwstraits.org.

How to explore the beach
without harming it

Low tides are wonderful times to explore the beach and discover all the fascinating creatures normally hidden from view. But at low tides they are especially vulnerable, exposed to sun and predators. We can easily damage them or their habitat.

We teach our children important lifetime values when we instill an ethic of respect and stewardship toward all life. It is better for beach critters if we leave them alone. Yet intertidal wildlife is more threatened by development, pollution, collecting, overharvesting and changing climate than from gentle touching by interested children and adults. With care we can minimize the risk to living creatures as we foster the sense of wonder that comes from touching a sea star's rough "skin," feeling a hermit crab crawl on our hand or looking eye-to-tentacle with an enormous moon snail.

We recommend the following beach etiquette be observed by adults and children:

- ✦ **Please leave** all living organisms where you find them. They are adapted to that habitat and may not survive in another place.
- ✦ **Walk with care** to avoid injuring plants and seaweeds – or yourself, because seaweeds are slippery. Beach plants prevent erosion. Seaweeds are living blankets that provide habitat and hiding places for many creatures from air, sun and predators. Eelgrass beds are nurseries for others. Step on bare spots if you can.
- ✦ **Kneel quietly by tidepools** and try not to walk in them.
- ✦ **Overturn rocks with care,** if doing so, then return them softly to their original position. Rock undersides are marine condominiums. If you leave uncovered the critters that live there, you destroy their home and possibly them, too. Lift only rocks smaller than your head, to avoid crushing the critters.
- ✦ **Touch animals gently** and avoid handling soft-bodied animals altogether. Sea stars are usually durable on their upper surface, but if you touch their tube feet they will attach to you and be torn off.
- ✦ **Enjoy anemones** without prodding them. Anemones often squirt water if poked, but this can kill them because they need that water for survival until the next tide covers them.
- ✦ **Leave attached** animals such as anemones, barnacles and mussels. Pulling and prying them from rocks or pilings will kill them.
- ✦ **Fill any holes** you dig. Piles of sand left on the beach can smother organisms beneath.
- ✦ **Leave the beach clean.** Bring a litterbag and carry out your own garbage as well as any trash you find, especially plastics, which are hazards to a variety of marine life.
- ✦ **Prevent pets** from harassing wildlife and carry out your pets' wastes as well.
- ✦ **Obtain permits** before harvesting any animals or plants. Obey limits set by fish and game laws, which are based on what we know from biology. Only by practicing conservation today will we leave this rich environment to future generations.

CHAPTER 3

Shoreline Access

What we left out

This book does not list every access to public tidelands. It omits some due to inadequate parking, safety concerns or difficult access. For information on public shoreline access sites not shown here, contact the Island County Planning and Community Development Department. Public tidelands accessible only from the water also are omitted. Check the Washington Department of Natural Resources website for the location of these tidelands.

Tides can prevent access

At high tide, many sites listed in this book do not allow access to beach walking on adjoining public tideland because high water reaches either private upland or the foot of a bluff. At low tide, exposed mud or sand flats at some sites may make it impossible to launch either trailered or hand-carried boats.

Finding the sites

To locate the sites listed in this book, use the map on pages 160-161 and the directions listed in the description for each site. We give driving instructions from state highways 20 and 525 for Whidbey, and from Terry's Corner for Camano. Visitors will find it helpful to refer to a driving map, available from Chambers of Commerce, visitor centers, realtors and many grocery stores. We abbreviate left, right, north, south, east and west as L, R, N, S, E and W.

Site descriptions

Coordinates: We include latitude and longitude coordinates for use with GPS units to help boaters find the public access when approaching from the water. We recorded these on shore near the water's edge except in a few cases where the road ends far from the shore. They are intended as a helpful guide. Do not rely on them for safe navigation.

Parking: 1, 2, 3, 4-6, etc. – parking for this number of vehicles. Sites with boat ramps offer limited parking for boat trailers. Most sites are restricted to day-use only. Overnight parking is available in major state parks. Public boat ramps and marinas may charge for launching or parking; check for fees and time limits before planning a trip. To park at Department of Fish & Wildlife accesses you must post a Vehicle Use Permit on your vehicle. Buy online or wherever hunting and fishing licenses are sold.

Symbols:

- Restroom with flush toilet
- Non-flush toilet (either portable or vault toilet)
- Potable water
- Picnic table(s)
- Covered picnic area
- Barbecue grill(s)
- Playground
- Dock or pier. Some are seasonal.
- Boat launch ramp, useable for both trailered and car-top boats. If site has a boat ramp, symbol for hand carried boat is not shown.
- No boat ramp is available, but car-top boats such as canoes and kayaks could be hand carried to water's edge. At sites with mudflats, water is reachable only at high tides.
- At least 600 feet of public tideland available for beach walking.
- A site considered a swimming beach
- A site used for fishing from shore
- A good site for bird watching
- Upland hiking trails at site
- Scenic view from parking area

Unlike most sites in this chapter, state parks offer nearly all the amenities. To save space we do not itemize every state park amenity. For this, see the Site Table on page 156. The table also lists additional features for many sites including boat moorage, kayak camps and barrier free access.

Adjoining public tideland: How far you can move along the beach before reaching private tideland, in linear feet. We researched this using county property records and descriptions. But the authors, publishers and sponsors cannot guarantee its accuracy. We did not conduct any boundary surveys.

WHIDBEY ISLAND SITES

Forty-five miles long and up to 10 miles wide, Whidbey is the longest island in the contiguous 48 states since a 1985 U.S. Supreme Court decision ruled New York state's Long Island is actually a peninsula.

Whidbey is reached at its north end by bridge and at its center and south end by ferry service. State Highway 20 connects to the island at Deception Pass Bridge and serves the north end. State Highway 525 connects at the ferry landing at Clinton and serves the south. The two highways meet at Wanamaker Road (called Race Road east of the highway), south of Coupeville. At this intersection Highway 525 ends and Highway 20 turns west on Wanamaker Road to the ferry landing at Keystone. Site directions on Whidbey Island are given from these state highways, which form the major north-south travel corridor.

NORTH WHIDBEY

Site 1 — **DECEPTION PASS STATE PARK**
Lat/Long: N 48° 24.004, W 122° 39.847

Directions: Turn W off Hwy 20 at stoplight 1 mile S of Deception Pass Bridge into park entrance, opposite Cornet Bay Rd.

The park provides excellent access to beaches and amenities. For information contact the state park (360-675-2417) or go to www.deceptionpassfoundation.org.

Washington's most popular state park, comprising 4,162 acres in Island and Skagit counties, Deception Pass State Park offers a breath-taking bridge, old growth forest, over 300 campsites, 10 kitchen shelters, two fresh water lakes, 10 boat ramps, 14 miles of shoreline, 40 miles of trails and kayaking, bird watching, clamming, crabbing, fresh and salt water swimming, scuba diving, fishing, sandy beaches, rugged cliffs and stunning views. In addition to the Whidbey Island sites described here, the park includes water access north of Deception Pass Bridge at Pass Lake, Bowman Bay and Rosario Head. Salt-water moorage is available at Cornet Bay and Bowman Bay. In the 1930s the Civilian Conservation Corps (CCC) built many of the roads, trails, buildings and bridges to develop the park. Some of the park trails are near steep banks and cliffs so be sure to carefully attend children.

When exploring the beaches of Deception Pass, keep in mind that six million feet walk the park each year. Human feet and probing hands can do more damage to intertidal areas than sub-zero temperatures on a low tide winter's night. Follow proper beach etiquette – cover up clam holes, return over-turned rocks to their original position, look with your eyes, not with your hands, and watch where you walk. Enjoy being a steward of the treasures nature created here. (Trail map p. 138)

Joseph Whidby discovers an island

It has been just over 200 years—only a few lifetimes—since Captain George Vancouver sailed into Puget Sound on the HMS Discovery. He anchored near Mukilteo and sent his ship's master, Joseph Whidby, to explore the inland waters later named Port Susan, Saratoga Passage and Skagit Bay. After exploring these inside waters, Whidby explored waters to the west. On June 10, 1792, he found an intricate and narrow, rocky channel leading into Skagit Bay, which he had earlier explored from

the inside. This confirmed he had been circumnavigating an island, which Vancouver named Whidby Island (later Whidbey) to honor the officer who discovered it. He named the narrow opening Deception Pass.

Deception Pass bridge

Site 2	CORNET BAY COUNTY DOCK

Lat/Long: N 48° 23.807, W 122° 37.868

Directions: 1 mile S of Deception Pass Bridge turn E onto Cornet Bay Rd. County dock is 1 mile on L at intersection of Cornet Bay Rd and Bay View Lane.

Parking: 10

Adjoining public tideland: 50 feet, lot width only.

Island County maintains this 120-foot dock for public moorage and hand-launching small boats. Fish or crab from the dock. Day use only. Contact Island County Parks Department for information about daily and annual moorage fees.

Site 3	**CORNET BAY BOAT LAUNCH** (Deception Pass State Park)
	Lat/Long: N 48° 24.064, W 122° 37.349

Directions: 1 mile S of Deception Pass Bridge turn E onto Cornet Bay Rd. State park facilities are 1.3 miles on L after private marina.

Parking: 110

Adjoining public tideland: None to west. To east 2.3 miles around Hoypus Point to southern park boundary.

Cornet Bay is a part of Deception Pass State Park, though private tidelands along the southern edge of the bay west of this access interrupt continuous state-owned tidelands. The park maintains a 6-lane deep-water boat ramp along with a dock, boat pump-out facility and showers. Fishers and crabbers are welcome to use the dock but boaters have priority for space. Ducks, cormorants and herons frequent the area. To the north is a clear view of lichen-covered bedrock and red-barked madrone trees on the slopes of Goose Rock. The summit is the highest point on Whidbey Island.

Dock next to Cornet Bay boat launch

Battle on the beach–intertidal zonation

Intertidal marine creatures on shorelines around the world must cope with a host of physical and biological challenges where the land meets the sea. As a result they have become grouped into distinct bands or zones. Intertidal zonation is most obvious on steep or rock-faced beaches where the horizontal tide range is small and the bands are narrow. It is less evident on flat beaches where the horizontal tide range can stretch hundreds of feet.

Zonation occurs partly because of local tidal conditions and partly because of the evolutionary and ecological makeup of individual plants and animals.

In general, quality of life in the upper tide zones depends on an animal's ability to manage physical conditions such as drying, temperature swings, fresh water dilution and wave action. In the lower tide zones the community is determined more by biological factors such as predators and the contest for space, food and mates.

Four common intertidal invertebrates (spineless creatures) illustrate how zonation works. Very high in the intertidal, a tiny brown barnacle, Chthamalus, *can take greater exposure to air and changing temperatures than most other invertebrates. It can also thrive much lower in the intertidal, but is not found there because a larger barnacle,* Balanus, *crowds out the little brown barnacle at lower levels.*

A snail, Nucella, *likes to eat the larger barnacle* Balanus, *but* Nucella *has more severe exposure limits and can only travel so far up into* Balanus *territory before it risks over-exposure.* Balanus *is safe from this predator as long as it does not dip into* Nucella *territory. Finally a low-intertidal species of sea star,* Pisaster, *is a voracious snail predator but does not do well when exposed to air for long periods. It eats* Nucella *snails that venture down into the sea star's territory, but* Pisaster *leaves alone snails that keep their proper distance higher in the mid-intertidal.*

Hundreds of such interactions take place along the intertidal shoreline, where the creatures of each zone live in an arrangement that allows them to meet their needs for growth and reproduction.

Atypical orange form of
Nucella lamellosa

Site 4	HOYPUS POINT (Deception Pass State Park)
	Lat/Long: N 48° 24.666, W 122° 36.427

Directions: (a) North entry and shore access–1 mile S of Deception Pass Bridge turn E onto Cornet Bay Rd and go 2.2 miles to parking area. Walk the final 0.25 mile to Hoypus Point. Access to trails is for walkers only from north side. (b) South entry to trails–Turn E onto Ducken Rd 0.25 mile S of Cornet Bay Rd. In 0.5 mile, where road curves sharp R, don't turn but continue straight ahead 0.3 mile to parking area. Mountain bikers and horseback riders can access trails here. Adjoins private property; drive slowly.

Parking: 8 at end of Cornet Bay Rd; 6 with horse trailers at end of Ducken Rd.

Adjoining public tideland: 1 mile S to park boundary; 1.3 miles NW to site 3.

(a) From the north parking area walk east on the former road to reach the shore access at Hoypus Point. Inland hiking trails through the forest reserve begin past a gate at the SE corner of the parking area and pass majestic old-growth Douglas firs 6 feet in diameter as well as huge western red cedars. (b) The Ducken Road entry provides trail access for horseback riders and mountain bikers. Various trails are restricted to hikers only; to hikers and horses; or to hikers, horses and mountain bikes; follow signs. (Trail map p. 139)

Site 5	ALA SPIT
	Lat/Long: N 48° 23.581, W 122° 35.200

Directions: Turn E off Hwy 20 at milepost 39.8 (2 miles S of Deception Pass Bridge) onto Troxell Rd. Travel 4 miles to Geck Rd. Drop down Geck Rd to road end and parking area.

Parking: 10-15

Adjoining public tideland: Tidelands either side of Ala Spit and in front of parking area.

This 12-acre site includes 1 mile of public beach, the 8-acre spit and 4 acres of uplands. Ala Spit is a narrow ridge of sand and gravel supplied by coastal erosion and transported by nearshore currents. The channel between the spit and Hope Island has provided excellent fishing grounds for recreational anglers. A diverse year-round bird population attracts bird watchers. This is a good place to look at plants found on our shorelines, from eelgrass beds along the beach to pickleweed on the inland mudflat and backshore plants (box, p.94) along the 1,800-foot trail to the end of the spit. South of the parking area is a kayak campsite.

Ala Spit

Eelgrass keeps the whole system going

Eelgrass is a nearshore treasure. Entire meadows of this grass-like peren-
nial grow in the shallows off many Island County beaches. It shelters
young salmon, forage fish and invertebrates (creatures with no spinal
column) by buffering the energy of waves and currents, and providing a
safe haven and nursery. Pacific herring lay their eggs on eelgrass. Salmon,
in turn, feast on the herring. Anemones, snails, stalked jellyfish, limpets
and nudibranchs anchor themselves to its long, green, ribbon-like leaves.
Clams and worms live in the soft sediments surrounding its roots.

Eelgrass grows by spreading its root system under the soft, sandy
substrate, and by underwater pollination and seed germination. It is one
of the very few true plants totally adapted to the marine environment
and receives nutrients through its roots and also directly from the water
column across its leaf surfaces. Its nutritional value is in the detritus (de-
caying plant litter) it produces. Like cheese spread on a cracker, eelgrass
becomes encrusted with a rich coating of diatoms, bacteria and protozoa.
When the plant dies back or is shredded by wave action, detritus-eating
organisms strip the leaf particles of their protein-rich microbial coatings.
A single piece of eelgrass detritus can be re-colonized by microbes and
passed again and again through the guts of invertebrates.

Recent, better understanding of the importance of eelgrass is lead-
ing to mapping and monitoring of eelgrass meadows and to conservation
measures to preserve them.

Site 6	**MORAN BEACH** (Powell Rd)
	Lat/Long: N 48° 22.386, W 122° 39.888

Directions: Turn W off Hwy 20 onto Banta Rd. Turn N onto Moran Rd, then W onto Powell Rd to road end, approximately 1 mile from Hwy 20.

Parking: 10-15+ 🚤🏕

Adjoining public tideland: 100 feet, directly in front of the paved parking lot and road end. Private tidelands to each side are well signed.

This sandy beach offers a sweeping view of the Strait of Juan de Fuca from the San Juan Islands to the Olympics. To the west is the low, flat profile of Smith Island, inhabited by eagles, seals and other wildlife.

Divers and dabblers dine differently

Each fall more than a dozen species of wintering ducks and seabirds arrive in our waters. Joining our familiar mallard and gadwall are wigeons, goldeneyes, scoters, loons and other species.

Watch closely how these species forage for food. Some dabble along the surface; others dive under the water to feed. The dabblers seek vegetation near the surface. Their horizontally flattened bills aid in filtering surface water as they feed along shallow edges. Dabblers include pintails, wigeons, shovelers and geese.

The category called divers submerge completely underwater using their feet and occasionally their wings for propulsion as they forage for swimming fish and also for invertebrates along the rocky bottom. These birds have narrow pointed bills to snatch fish and to poke around looking for invertebrates. Our many divers include buffleheads, goldeneyes, scoters, mergansers, cormorants, grebes, loons and guillemots.

Watch for dabblers and divers. Knowing these categories will help you find the birds in guides and zero in on identifying unfamiliar species.

Site 7	**DUGUALLA BAY DIKE ACCESS**
	Lat/Long: N 48° 21.398, W 122° 35.891

Directions: Turn E off Hwy 20 onto Frostad Rd. In 0.8 mile turn N onto Dike Rd, go up onto dike and park along wide shoulder on E side at midpoint of dike, across from pump station. Note: pull-off south of dike is on private land.

Parking: 5 🚤🚶🐦🏕

Adjoining public tideland: To north 1.5 miles.

This access once had a county boat ramp on the salt water side, but it long since disappeared under gravel. From the north end of the dike you can walk the shore along Department of Natural Resources (DNR) Beach 145 below a steep bluff. At low tides the bay east of the dike becomes a ¼-mile-long mudflat with rich feeding for birds. A large expanse of fresh water inside the dike provides habitat for waterfowl and shorebirds. This site lies under one of the main approaches to Whidbey Island Naval Air Station to the west, so you could be surprised by low-flying aircraft.

Site 8 — DUGUALLA STATE PARK
Lat/Long: N 48° 20.400, W 122° 34.333

Directions: From Hwy 20 turn E onto Sleeper Rd, go 2.6 miles to road end and gate at park boundary.

Parking: 4

Adjoining public tideland: 6,690 feet.

This 600-acre unimproved area, formerly DNR School Trust Forest land, is accessible only on foot. It's a 1½-mile walk to the shore. From the gate, follow the single-lane dirt road to a Y, take right fork ¼ mile to another Y, take left fork, and in ¼ mile reach road end. From here a trail winds steeply downhill past some enormous old trees to the beach. The park has nearly 1¼ miles of public shoreline, though at high tides much of the beach is covered by water and is unwalkable. Sections of this shaded beach provide ideal spawning habitat for forage fish. Hiding in the uplands of the park is Sleeper Bog, where a careful explorer may discover plants that are bog specialists. For information about this area contact Deception Pass State Park (360-675-2417). Day use only.

Overhanging trees help fish eggs survive

Trees and brush at the base of eroding beach slopes often reach out toward the water at a nearly horizontal angle. This can make it difficult to walk the beach at high tide, tempting landowners to cut the overhanging vegetation. But if left in place, these trees provide priceless shading and cooling of the beach gravels, greatly improving survival of forage fish eggs that would otherwise be killed by harsh midday temperatures. On a sunny day, shoreside cover can keep the beach surface as much as 10° F cooler than a bare beach. Native vegetation on bluff slopes also helps to stabilize the bluff, reducing the threat of landslides.

Site 9	**BORGMAN ROAD END**
	Lat/Long: N 48° 19.361, W 122° 31.360

Directions: From N of Oak Harbor, turn off Hwy 20 onto Fakkema Rd, then S onto Taylor Rd. In 0.8 mile turn E onto Silver Lake Rd, travel 3.5 miles, then go N onto Green Rd for 0.25 mile, then E onto Borgman Rd and down short slope to road end. From downtown Oak Harbor, go E on Pioneer Way, turn L onto Regatta Rd, then E onto Crescent Harbor Rd. In 2 miles turn N onto Taylor Rd, and in 0.25 mile E onto Silver Lake Rd. Follow remaining directions above.

Parking: 2

Adjoining public tideland: Width of roadway only.

This site provides easy access for kayak and canoe boaters to launch their craft, with a low level vista of Mt. Baker and the Skagit Delta. The site is surrounded by residential development, so please respect the privacy of those who live there.

Site 10	**MARINERS COVE BOAT RAMP**
	Lat/Long: N 48° 17.408, W 122° 31.090

Directions: From Hwy 20 or Pioneer Way turn onto Regatta Rd. Turn E onto Crescent Harbor Rd. In 3.5 miles road turns S and becomes Reservation Rd, then in another 1.5 miles turns E and becomes Polnell Rd. After another 2.5 miles, where Polnell becomes Strawberry Point Rd, turn E downhill onto Mariners Beach Dr. Follow 0.4 mi to public access on the L before end of Mariners Beach Dr; a loop gravel pullout with lawn, bench and small boat launch.

Parking: 4

Adjoining public tideland: 245 feet.

Drift log buildup may block the small boat ramp. The view sweeps from Mt. Baker to Glacier Peak and the Skagit Delta. Utsalady Point on Camano Island is 2 miles across the water to the south. The waters along this beach often run muddy, especially after a heavy rainfall, due to sediment flowing from the North Fork of the Skagit River. The Skagit River accounts for 38% of sediment discharge in the Puget Sound lowland, with sediment runoff peaking in late winter and late spring. This access has close neighbors and requires special attention and respect for private property.

Mariners Cove Boat Ramp

Crustacean molts—the shell game

That "dead crab" on the beach may not be the last remains of the deceased. If you have ever dined on freshly-cooked crab or shrimp you know about the rigid outer covering that must be removed before getting to the delicious sweet meat. This outer covering or exoskeleton is secreted by the epidermis and hardens into the animal's shell-like support structure.

As crustaceans grow, every so often they must shed their exoskeleton and replace it with a larger one—a process called molting. As the animal prepares to molt it secretes a new, soft cuticle under its outer shell. The old shell splits along specific break points and the entire animal wriggles out, down to the last tiny claw and even the cuticle covering the eyeball.

Right after molting, while in the "soft shell" stage, the animal pumps itself full of water to stretch the new soft cuticle into a larger covering. After the new shell has been hardened with calcium taken up from seawater, the water is pumped out and replaced by animal tissue as the crustacean grows. Young animals molt several times a year; older animals less often, or they may stop molting.

On the beach, molted exoskeletons often are mistaken for dead animals. To find out whether an empty skeleton is a molt or a dead animal, smell it! A molt will have only the fresh smell of the seashore.

Site 11   OAK HARBOR CITY MARINA (a.k.a. Catalina Shores Marine Park)
Lat/Long: N 48° 17.115, W 122° 37.917

Directions: Located in the City of Oak Harbor. Turn E off Hwy 20 onto Pioneer Way. Travel 1.2 miles, turning R into marina on Catalina Dr just before entry booth to Navy Seaplane Base. For boat launch, drive past storage sheds, then turn R toward water.

Parking: 50+ 🚻🅿️🚲⛱️📷🛶🚤🛥️🐟🎣🚶

Adjoining public tideland: Approximately 0.5 mile.

The marina has a very limited beach area to walk, but a paved footpath above the shoreline connects to sites 12-14. The entire marina is open to the public, including the docks which have picnic tables at the ends. A play and picnic area is north of the park office. A small park next to the boat ramp at the south end of the property is a great place from which to watch the harbor activity. From February to May, in a partnership between the City of Oak Harbor and Washington Department of Fish & Wildlife, coho salmon fingerlings are raised at the marina in net pens. The salmon released each spring provide a local fishery when they return in autumn two years later.

Oak Harbor City Marina

Site 12   PIONEER WAY EAST
Lat/Long: N 48° 17.379, W 122° 38.313

Directions: Located in old downtown Oak Harbor. Turn E off Hwy 20 onto Pioneer Way and proceed 0.5 mile past commercial district to waterside parking. Park along the road and access the beach via the stairs.

Parking: Along street 🚶🐟🎣🚶

Adjoining public tideland: 644 feet opposite Pasek St.

East of the intersection with Bayshore Drive, a sidewalk parallels the shore beside Pioneer Way. Extensive mudflats are exposed at low tide, accessed by stairways. The shorefront has mixed ownership, with some sections belonging to homeowners across the street. Please respect any stairs posted private. Spartina, a destructive non-native grass, has invaded this waterfront and is being fought by community volunteers.

Pioneer Way East

Spartina grass, a destructive shoreline invader

Spartina is a halophyte, meaning it is a terrestrial plant adapted to grow in salt water. As an invasive species it is an unwelcome newcomer to Island County beaches. In the 1960s, farmers planted what they believed to be sterile hybrid seed along tidelands in an attempt to increase the amount of land where their cattle could graze. Unfortunately, the seed was not sterile and began spreading throughout the area, eventually infesting thousands of acres.

Also known as cord grass, spartina utterly transforms the ecosystem, displacing native vegetation and raising the elevation of the area where it establishes. Its dense root system traps sediment, turning eelgrass beds and mudflats into grass-choked marsh. It is a grave threat to native fish, shellfish and migrating shorebirds. Once established, it is very difficult to remove. The aggressive spread of spartina grass in Willapa Bay on the Washington coast has reduced by 50 percent the number of shorebirds feeding at this important migration stop.

Public and private agencies are working hard to eradicate this noxious weed. To contact the Island County Noxious Weed Control Board, call 360-240-5597 or visit the office of Washington State University Extension of Island County in Coupeville.

Site 13   FLINTSTONE PARK (a.k.a. Mini Harbor Park)
Lat/Long: N 48° 17.223, W 122° 38.846

Directions: Located in the City of Oak Harbor. Turn E off Hwy 20 onto Pioneer Way and turn S onto SE City Beach St, then E on Bayshore Dr. Park is on S side after Dock St.

Parking: Along street 🚻🚮🏕🏠✏🚶🛶🚤

Adjoining public tideland: 415 feet.

This quiet park and "mini harbor" provides an excellent view of the Oak Harbor Marina. Sit on the sandy beach with the ducks and watch the boat traffic in the harbor. Seasonal docks provide platforms for fishing and day-use moorage for shallow-draft boats. Watch out for tides that can leave a boat stranded.

Flintstone Park

Site 14   WINDJAMMER PARK (a.k.a. City Beach)
Lat/Long: N 48° 17.137, W 122° 39.081

Directions: Located in the City of Oak Harbor. West entrance: Turn S onto Beeksma Dr at stoplight where Hwy 20 makes 90° turn west. This provides access to boat ramp and campground. East entrance: Turn E off Hwy 20 onto Pioneer Way. Turn S onto SE City Beach St and continue straight into parking area, close to playground, swimming lagoon and waterside picnic tables.

Parking: 50+ 🚻🚮🏕🖼🚣🛶🚶🛥🚤🚶🏕

Adjoining public tideland: 2,380 feet.

This popular family park has a swimming lagoon, playground equipment, ball fields and a campground. The boat ramp is tide limited; consider deep-water ramp at site 11. A paved footpath follows the shoreline, stretching 1½ miles from Beeksma Dr to the marina. The view spans past the mouth of Penn Cove down Saratoga Passage, and east above the masts of moored boats to the distant snow-capped Cascades. West from Beeksma Dr, a graveled trail crosses Freund's Marsh to a parking area for 6-8 cars at Scenic Heights Rd. See p. 140 for a map of the waterfront trail and a walking tour of the city's splendid old Garry oak trees. For more information on Sites 11-14, contact Oak Harbor Public Works Department, 360-279-4752.

Before the bridge

Just one of many early ferry services in Island County was the Oak Harbor–Utsalady ferry that ran from 1925–1935, linking the county's two populated islands much more directly than today's three-county drive. The ferry Acorn was owned by the husband-wife team of Agaton and Berte Olson, who also operated the Deception Pass Ferry. Berte Olson was the stuff of legends, becoming Washington's first licensed female ferry boat skipper. From the arrival of the first white settlers in the 1850s until completion of the Deception Pass Bridge in 1935, transportation in Island County was focused on the water. Early maritime transportation took place in sailing ships and canoes with hired crews of Indians to paddle them, but during the Mosquito Fleet era it shifted to sternwheelers, side-wheelers and propeller-driven ships. Many early communities, such as Langley, did a thriving business supplying wood to keep the boilers going on these steam-powered vessels.

The Acorn, circa 1925.

ROCKY POINT PICNIC AREA (U.S. Navy)
Lat/Long: N 48° 19.348, W 122° 42.084

Directions: From Hwy 20, W onto Ault Field Rd. In 2 miles continue W
on Clover Valley Rd (where main route turns sharp L onto Heller). After 0.8
mile turn R toward Rocky Point Picnic Area and Archery Range. Drive all
the way to end, beyond pavement down to graveled beach parking area. Walk
across 100 feet of drift logs to reach a wide sandy beach.

Parking: 10+ 🚻 ⛵ 🏖 🚶

Adjoining public tideland: South 0.5 mile to Joseph Whidbey State Park.

This sand beach, property of the U.S. Navy, is open to anyone with a Department of Defense U.S. Uniformed Services ID card. Others wanting permission to walk the beach may send a letter to the Base Commanding Officer.
The beach meets Joseph Whidbey State Park to the south. There is a live
firing range between, so pay attention to warning flags and signs.

Mother seals leave pups on the beach while they hunt

*Every year someone comes upon an adorable seal pup on the beach and thinks
it's been abandoned. With good intentions they do all the wrong things.
Harbor seal birthing season in our region runs from late June through the end
of August. A newborn pup isn't strong enough to keep up while mom hunts
in the sea, so the mother seal leaves it behind for periods of time till it reaches
about four to six weeks of age. After hunting, the mother returns to nurse and
protect it—unless people have interfered. Human activity around the young
animal can cause a mother seal to abandon her pup, in which case it surely
will die. That's why it's against federal law to disturb any marine mammal
or come within 100 feet of its location. By far the best way to help a pup is to
leave it alone. It does not need to be encouraged back into the sea nor kept wet,
and the last thing it needs is to be removed from the beach! Seals and other
marine mammals sometimes carry diseases transmissible to humans, pets and
livestock, yet another reason to keep people and dogs away. If a pup is on a
beach where it may be disturbed, volunteers from the Central Puget Sound
Marine Mammal Stranding Network will post signs warning people to leave
it alone. To report a stranded seal pup or other marine mammal, call (Whidbey) 1-360-678-3765 or 1-866-ORCANET, (Camano) 1-360-387-8299.
To report harassment of a seal pup or other marine mammal, call the NOAA
Enforcement Hotline at 1-800-853-1964.*

Site 16 | JOSEPH WHIDBEY STATE PARK
Lat/Long: N 48° 18.471, W 122° 42.986

Directions: From Oak Harbor turn W off Hwy 20 onto Swantown Rd. Travel 3 miles to stop sign at T intersection with Crosby Rd. The state park entrance is opposite on N side of Crosby. There are two other parking areas with no facilities: (a) turn L to public beach access at bottom of hill immediately N of first residence, where West Beach Rd turns S; or (b) turn R onto Crosby Rd for 0.75 mile; Crosby curves L, then R, and entrance to unpaved parking area is on NW side on second curve. From north Whidbey, follow directions to site 15, continuing on Clover Valley Rd, which becomes Golf Course Rd. At T turn R on Crosby Rd to the park.

Parking: 25+ 🚻🅿️⛩🏠📊⚓🎣🏃🏄🚶🚴🏕

Adjoining public tideland: Northward 3,100 feet to park boundary. Beyond is the beach adjoining Rocky Point Picnic Area (site 15).

Joseph Whidbey State Park

Expansive water views, sandy beach walking and picnic sites are the main attractions at 112-acre Joseph Whidbey State Park, which is open for day use only. Administered by Fort Ebey State Park, this site has limited amenities and parking. Facilities include fields for badminton, soccer and volleyball, and 2 miles hiking and biking trails. This is a popular site for sailboarding. A Washington Water Trails water-access-only campsite is located at the northern-most corner of the lower lawn (the only camping allowed in the park). Park facilities are closed Oct. 1-Mar. 31 but the park is open for day use; year-round parking is available at the two alternate parking areas.

Walk the long sand beach or the trail through beach grass inland of the driftwood which passes a marsh at the north end. The low profile of Smith and Minor islands, which are joined at low tide, can be seen four miles offshore in the Strait of Juan de Fuca. A mile-long loop trail through forest and field can be reached from the main paved parking area or from the east parking area on Crosby Rd. The park offers diverse birding opportunities, with forest and grassland habitats, a wetland by the north boundary, marine birds offshore, and Swan Lake (a.k.a Bos Lake) south of the park. (Trail map p. 141)

Site 17 WEST BEACH VISTA (a.k.a. Sunset Beach)
Lat/Long: N 48° 17.908, W 122° 43.486

Directions: Follow directions for Joseph Whidbey State Park. Continue 0.8 miles S on West Beach Rd, paralleling the shore between a row of residences to W and Swan Lake to E. South of the houses, park on W side of road in pull-off near large chunks of broken concrete wall or up hill at fenced overlook.
Parking: 9

Adjoining public tideland: To south 1.85 miles.

This unimproved site under Island County ownership is a popular place to watch the sunset. It's also a good place to witness the limits of man's ability to control nature. A huge concrete seawall lies in ruins here, left from a failed attempt to create beachfront property along a dynamic (moving) shoreline.

Shoreline alterations—death by a thousand cuts

In the two centuries since Europeans first sailed into these waters, humans have introduced a great variety of manmade materials to the shoreline in an effort to alter and control nature. These include bulkheads, groins, pilings, concrete ramps, steel rails, over-water piers, stairways and rubber tires. Often these are poorly planned, unneeded or built without an understanding of natural processes, resulting in failure of the structure, habitat destruction or accelerated erosion of the beach on either side. These structures can interfere with normal sediment transport, making beaches unusable to forage fish that would otherwise lay thousands of eggs on them. They may prevent sunlight from penetrating into the photic zone, causing eelgrass to stop growing. They may leach carcinogenic chemicals onto beaches, water and sediments, endangering both marine life and humans. Such damage is especially sad if the structure was never needed in the first place, is no longer needed, or could have been designed to minimize damage. Between 2002 and 2004 the Island County Marine Resources Committee and WSU Beach Watchers mapped the locations of these structures on every foot of county shoreline and entered this information into a database. By combining these data with other shoreline information, a picture is emerging of how these materials affect beach erosion, eelgrass beds, forage fish spawning activities and other processes.

HASTIE LAKE BOAT RAMP
Lat/Long: N 48° 15.874, W 122° 44.882

Directions: Turn W off Hwy 20 onto Hastie Lake Rd. Follow Hastie Lake Rd 2.5 miles across West Beach Rd to road end and County Park. From the south get to sites 16-18 by turning W off Hwy 20 onto Libbey Rd, then N onto West Beach Rd. From intersection of Libbey Rd and West Beach, site 18 is 2.25 miles, site 17 is 4.9 miles, and site 16 is 5.7 miles.

Parking: 10

Adjoining public tideland: Below Meander Line, 700 feet to north and 5 miles south to site 20. This is a site where the Meander Line is somewhat marked on the low tide as the line created between the sandy beach and the cobblestones. Walk only on the cobblestoned area to access public tidelands as you move north and south.

Enjoy a view of the Olympic Mountains, Vancouver Island and San Juans. An "ADA" parking site offers bench access next to boat ramp. The boat ramp is limited to use during conditions of slack water and no winds. Excessive seaweed harvesting has occurred in the area. Recent laws restrict the amount that can be taken. Walk the beach southward below towering bluffs, but be cautious about tide levels. In places, waves at high tide reach the foot of the bluffs; don't get trapped. This access has close neighbors. Please pay attention and respect private property.

Much of the glacial material of this beach originated from igneous, metamorphic and sedimentary rocks of the coastal mountains in British Columbia. The larger rocks provide a measure of erosion protection because they dissipate wave energy.

Nature shows us how to live on bluffs and shorelines

Educational programs such as Island County Shore Stewards and WSU Beach Watchers are helping shoreline property owners learn more natural ways to manage their land and bluffs. Many are adopting practices for their gardens, homes and beaches that help preserve groundwater, reduce runoff, use fewer chemicals and pesticides, accommodate natural erosion and help stabilize slopes with native bluff vegetation and drought-resistant plants. They are applying the principles of Low-Impact Development to help the land absorb rainfall rather than drain it away, and making smarter use of natural hydrology and soil processes to provide healthier habitat for marine life and other creatures.

Site 19 MONROE LANDING
Lat/Long: N 48° 14.421, W 122° 40.836

Directions: From the north, turn S off Hwy 20 onto Monroe Landing Rd. Follow this road almost 2 miles to road end. The park is directly in front of you, with a gravel lot for boat trailers across the street. From the south, turn E off Hwy 20 onto Arnold Rd to Monroe Landing Rd, then turn R to end as above.

Parking: 8 ▱ 🚶 🏕

Adjoining public tideland: 0.5 mile to east, none to the west

Monroe Landing, located on Penn Cove across from the town of Coupeville, offers a striking view of the Olympic mountain range. At low tide on this sandy beach you can easily locate the burrows of ghost shrimp (box, p. 72). As early as 1300 the Skwdabs, a subgroup of the Skagit, had a permanent settlement, Cokwol'a, at what is now called Monroe Landing. Their territory also included Oak Harbor and Dugualla Bay. They had a potlatch house at Monroe Landing until the early 1900s, and surrounding tribes would travel in canoes to attend gift-giving ceremonies. The site at Monroe Landing was the last of the longhouses (potlatch houses) on Whidbey and was constructed atop a midden about 4,000 years old.

Monroe Landing

The Coast Salish peoples

Centuries before Europeans arrived in their tall ships, Coast Salish peoples fished, hunted, gathered shellfish and berries, built plank houses and traveled by canoe among permanent and seasonal villages throughout the Pacific Northwest, including British Columbia. Clovis spear points found at prehistoric sites in Penn Cove were used in hunting the woolly mammoth, which roamed Whidbey Island after the last ice age. This indicates humans have inhabited central Whidbey for over 10,000 years. Thirty-four archeological sites have been found on Penn Cove alone, including three permanent Salish villages.

Families intermarried over a large area and participated in a potlatch economic system where resources were regularly shared. At Ebey's Prairie on Whidbey Island they encouraged root crops such as bracken fern and camas through selective burning. They trapped salmon in nearby rivers and harvested shellfish from Penn Cove. In addition, they hunted game, and harvested wild potatoes, berries and other plants. The area's bountiful resources produced a natural surplus of many foods, enabling the Salish to develop social organization that went beyond foraging to accommodate specialists. This surplus also allowed for the large populations and permanent village sites found in most of the sheltered coves on the lee side of the islands.

Puget Sound Coast Salish used a distinctive weaving style that included the use of dog fur, mountain goat wool and plant fibers. They are also known for their carving and sophisticated basket weaving. European diseases took a staggering toll after first contact. In January 1855, Puget Sound Coast Salish leaders signed the Treaty of Point Elliot with Governor Isaac Stevens and ceded their lands. Laws were passed making traditional economic and religious practices of the Coast Salish illegal. Speaking the Coast Salish language was also forbidden in schools, and other attempts at cultural assimilation occurred. Today, many Coast Salish people are reclaiming their traditional heritage while living in the modern world and making use of modern resources. The Penn Cove Water Festival, with its popular Native canoe races, celebrates and honors this long heritage.

Site 20	LIBBEY BEACH PARK
	Lat/Long: N 48° 13.925, W 122° 46.011

Directions: Turn W off Hwy 20 onto Libbey Rd and follow 1.2 miles to road end.

Parking: 10 [icons][when reopens] [icons]

Adjoining public tideland: 5 miles to north and 3 miles to south. Tidelands to the north are from Meander Line to the Extreme Low Tide extending to Hastie Lake site. Tidelands to the south are from Ordinary High Water to Extreme Low Tide. With 8 miles of beach to walk, keep track of time and tides. A high tide could leave you stranded, wet or hanging from the bluff.

Eroding bluffs along this stretch of west Whidbey provide constant nourishment for the wide sand beaches several miles north. *Due to erosion and liability concerns, beach access from this site is currently closed and is not slated to reopen until 2008.* The upland amenities and expansive view from this 3-acre park remain. This area, also known as Partridge Point is a great place for winter birding looking out over the strait. For information on access reopening, contact Island County Parks Department.

Libbey Beach Park

Forest of the seas—phytoplankton and seaweeds

A secret world lies just beneath the cold waters of the Pacific Northwest—a smorgasbord of seaweeds growing in layers much like a terrestrial forest of trees, shrubs and ground covers. Moreover, the entire marine forest is bathed seasonally in a rich soup of single-celled algae called phytoplankton.

The forest canopy. Large, fast-growing kelps form the tree or canopy layer. Nereocystis, commonly known as bull kelp, can grow up to five inches in one day and reach heights of over 30 feet in one growing season.

The shrub layer. Below the kelps are shorter multi-branching foliose and filamentous seaweeds, the shrub layer.

The marine ground covers. Below the shrubs are the marine ground covers—seaweeds that form carpet-like coverings or thin crusts over rocks. Each layer of the marine forest has its own complement of fish and invertebrate species.

Like their terrestrial counterparts, seaweeds and single-celled phytoplankton form the base of the Earth's food web. They use chlorophyll and other accessory pigments to harness the sun's energy and convert carbon dioxide and water into sugar molecules. Phytoplankton is found throughout the world's oceans suspended in the water column. Seaweeds attach themselves to rocks and most are restricted to the shallow depths of shoreline that meet their sunlight requirements for growth.

Seaweeds do not have roots or nutrient transport systems like eelgrass and other true plants. They attach themselves to rocks with "holdfasts" and use their suspended blades to extract nutrients directly from the water column. Like eelgrass, the main food benefit from seaweeds is in the detritus, pieces of dead or dying tissue encrusted with protein-rich mats of microbes, which are consumed by detritus eaters.

Phytoplankton and seaweeds grow rapidly starting in spring (an event referred to as the spring bloom), then die back during fall and winter when there are fewer hours of daylight. Some seaweeds are perennials, surviving more than two years. Others are annuals, renewing themselves each spring.

Phytoplankton and seaweed blooms can also be destructive to marine habitats, smothering invertebrates and other seaweeds, and depleting the water of oxygen as they decay. Harmful algal blooms are being reported more frequently around the world, and pollution from inadequately treated sewage, agricultural run-off, erosion, and waste from animals, including pets, seems to be a major source of excess nutrients that cause such blooms.

| Site 21 | **FORT EBEY STATE PARK**
Lat/Long: N 48° 13.548, W 122° 46.000 |

Directions: Turn W off Hwy 20 onto Libbey Rd. Follow Libbey Rd 0.75 mile and turn S onto Hill Valley Dr. Follow 0.75 mile to state park entrance. For beach access, take road N to parking for beach and lake trails 0.5 mile beyond entry booth.

The park provides most amenities. For information contact the state park (360-678-4636) or go to **www.parks.wa.gov.**

The 645-acre park, with three miles of saltwater shoreline on the Strait of Juan de Fuca, is open year-round for camping and day use. Fort Ebey was constructed in 1942 for coastal defense. Adjoining the park to the east is an area known for its "kettles," large depressions in the earth left as the last glaciers receded. The park and surrounding area features more than 28 miles of trails for hiking and mountain biking. Horseback riding is allowed on those trails in the Kettles area that are not on state park land. Visitors may also explore concrete bunkers and gun batteries, surf, para-glide, or fish for smallmouth bass in Lake Pondilla.

The beach can be accessed at the north end of the park by the Beach Parking Lot and the restroom or via a trail and stairs down the bluff at the south end of the park. You can walk along the beach as far as Fort Casey, about eight miles. Check tides before departing, as high tides can trap you between water and bluff. A single Wash. Water Trails campsite is at the south end of the day-use area near the north Beach Parking Lot. (Trail map p. 142)

| Site 22 | **GRASSER'S LAGOON**
Lat/Long: N 48° 14.042, W 122° 43.925 |

Directions: On S side of Hwy 20 at the NW corner of Penn Cove, 100 ft W of Zylstra Rd and 0.25 mile E of Madrona Way, turn into U-shaped gravel pullout.

Parking: 8-10 🚤 🚶 🐟 🎣
Adjoining public tideland: To west and south 2,640 feet

A Washington Vehicle Use Permit (from WDFW) is required to park here. At minus tides the mudflats south of the lagoon are popular with clam diggers. Be aware of the tides. Bald eagles and kingfishers frequent the area, and shorebirds and ducks forage in the lagoon.

Before you dig!

To determine if the beach where you plan to dig is currently open and safe for shellfish harvesting, call the state Paralytic Shellfish Poisoning (PSP) Hotline at 1-800-562-5632 and the Island County Health Department at 360-679-7350 (from S. Whidbey 360-321-5111 ext. 7350; from Camano Island 360-629-4522 ext. 7350).

Buy a license from Washington Department of Fish & Wildlife (WDFW) and wear it while harvesting. Check and follow regulations for seasons, size limits and harvest limits. Refill holes after digging. Respect private property and harvest only within public beach boundaries. For more information on Island County clamming beaches and sustainable harvesting see page 118.

© Sally Slotterback

Site 23   WEST PENN COVE ACCESS
Lat/Long: N 48° 13.452, W 122° 43.858

Directions: From Hwy 20 turn S onto Madrona Way along W end of Penn Cove. Go 0.8 mile to the access, a U-shaped gravel pullout on the E side of Madrona Way about 0.1 mile N of the Captain Whidbey Inn. Note the WDFW sign.

Parking: 6

Adjoining public tideland: North for about 2,000 feet and south about 0.5 mile around Captain Whidbey Inn.

A Washington Vehicle Use Permit from WDFW is required to park here. This beach has been stocked with shellfish by WDFW. Much of the beach surrounds the Captain Whidbey Inn complex. Please respect the privacy of the hotel guests.

West Penn Cove Access

Penn Cove mussel rafts

Many visitors to the Coupeville area are puzzled by dozens of small rafts anchored in neat rows along the south shore of Penn Cove. These are part of a major aquaculture farm, Penn Cove Shellfish, LLC. Lines are suspended from the rafts and mussels grow on these lines until they are hoisted from the water and the mussels harvested. Thanks to an accident of geography, Penn Cove serves as a nutrient trap for outflows from the Skagit and Stillaguamish rivers. The influx of fresh water, combined with sunshine from the rain-shadow effect of the Olympic Mountains, fills Penn Cove with a "plankton soup" ideal for growing mussels. Penn Cove Shellfish also wet-stores and distributes oysters and clams, but over the course of several decades has really made its name worldwide for mussels.

Site 24	COUPEVILLE TOWN PARK
	Lat/Long: N 48° 13.271, W 122° 41.531

Directions: Located in Coupeville uphill from the wharf. From Hwy 20 turn N onto Main St. In 0.5 mile turning W with the main route onto Coveland St. After crossing Alexander, the road goes uphill. As it veers L, the park entrance is on the R at the corner of NW Colburn.

Parking: 12 🧑‍🤝‍🧑🚻♿🪑🎪⛱️🥏🚶

Adjoining public tideland: To east 0.5 mile.

The park offers broad grassy lawns, a children's play area, picnic facilities and a gazebo where outdoor concerts are held on summer Sundays. A kiosk holds an enormous slice of a 700-year-old Douglas fir which was a sapling about 200 years before Columbus arrived in America. From the north side, a gravel trail descends in switchbacks down the bluff to the beach. When beach walking, be aware that waves reach the base of the bluff at high tides.

Ebey's Landing National Historical Reserve

The tug of history is everywhere on central Whidbey Island. The picturesque seaside village of Coupeville, with its false-front buildings and historic wharf, sits only a short distance from rich natural prairies and woodlands dotted with turn-of-the-century homes and working farms, sweeping vistas of mountains and sea, old frontier blockhouses and a marvelous pioneer cemetery. Equally important is what is not there—urban sprawl and built-up development. Central Whidbey's natural beauty and historic roots have been preserved for future generations by a unique experiment—the 17,400-acre Ebey's Landing National Historical Reserve. This first-of-its-kind national park is built on the concept of maintaining mostly private ownership and use of the land, while employing tax incentives and other strategies to preserve its character. Today, some farmers of central Whidbey still work land claims that date back in their families to the mid-1800s.

COUPEVILLE WHARF & BEACH ACCESSES
Lat/Long: N 48° 13.277, W 122° 41.298

Directions: Located on the Coupeville waterfront. From Hwy 20 turn N onto Main St and W onto Coveland. In 2 blocks turn N onto Alexander, go 1 block to wharf.

Parking: Extensive parking along adjoining streets. Wharf is wheelchair-accessible. 🚻🅿️🚌🛶🎣🚶🛥️

Adjoining public tideland: 0.5 mile.

A 500-foot walkway leads to the wharf building and dock facilities, owned and operated by the Port of Coupeville (360-678-5020). Marine life exhibits and marine mammal skeletons are on display. Once the heart of Whidbey Island, Coupeville was served by regular Mosquito Fleet steam boat service from the 1890s to 1937, connecting it with Seattle, Everett and many small towns (box p. 90). During lower tides abundant sea life may be visible from the wharf including barnacles, mussels, jellyfish and sea stars. The shoreline can be accessed by stairways at the foot of the wharf and two blocks east at the foot of Main Street.

© Joan Gerteis

Coupeville Wharf

Birds of the beach

Select any beach around Island County and you might see these birds as you stroll. The most common will likely be gulls—perched on pilings, standing on mudflats or floating on the bay. If you see a gull standing in shallow water, watch closely and you may observe it "treading" the sand to stir up invertebrates for lunch. A family of crows might fly past or call from overhanging trees. A bald eagle could be perched high on a snag or sitting right on the beach. Gulls, crows and eagles all scavenge tidbits washed in by the last high tide. Both gulls and crows carry shellfish into the air, then drop them onto rocks or pavement to crack the shells and reach the meat inside.

A group of killdeer might scamper along the sandy beach. If you approach too closely they'll voice a warning. Above them a belted kingfisher might fire its loud rattling call as it flies up and down the beach. In winter watch for flocks of sanderlings, a small shorebird with pale gray back, pure white belly and coal black legs, eyes and bill, chasing waves on sandy beaches in a blur of running feet. Stand still and they may pass close by you.

Out on the water, especially in winter, you can see groups of ducks and seabirds. These could be scoters, buffleheads, goldeneyes, wigeons, scaups and grebes. You might even see a black and white loon swimming along, then diving underwater to seek prey.

Site 26   CAPTAIN COUPE PARK
Lat/Long: N 48° 13.240, W 122° 40.715

Directions: Located in Coupeville. From Hwy 20 turn N onto Main St and E onto 9th St. Go six blocks, turn into park on N side of road immediately past sewage treatment plant. An RV dump station is at top of drive.
Parking: 8 🚻🚮🅿️🖼️🚣🛶🎣🏕️♿

Adjoining public tideland: 1.6 miles east to Long Point.

Boat launching and retrieval can be a problem due to strong northwest winds. At low tide the dock sits atop mudflats. The tidelands here are typical for inland waters that have low wave impacts. Mudflats are filled with clams and other burrowing organisms, and surface substrates support barnacle and mussel communities. The area is known for spawning smelt and supports limited eelgrass beds. A roadside pedestrian trail running from Captain Coupe Park to the Front Street commercial district offers views and resting benches.

Captain Coupe Park

Salmon cruise the eelgrass highway

Island County sits at the center of Puget Sound, on the migration corridors used by salmon from nearly all of Puget Sound's major river systems. The many pocket estuaries and eelgrass beds on both sides of the islands provide critical shelter and refuge from predators and high-energy marine environments. Migrating salmon feed on herring, which lay their eggs directly on the eelgrass. Salmon also consume surf smelt and sand lance, which spawn on the gravels of Island County's many healthy beaches. Because healthy beaches and eelgrass beds are so important to the entire marine food chain, Island County Marine Resources Committee (MRC) and WSU Beach Watchers have been working for several years to survey and inventory critical nearshore resources.

Together with Island County Shore Stewards, they are helping the public understand how we can help preserve and protect these precious natural resources for future generations.

© Mary Jo Adams

LONG POINT
Lat/Long: N 48° 13.575, W 122° 38.941

Directions: From Hwy 20 at Coupeville turn N onto Main St and E onto 9th St which becomes Parker Rd. Travel approximately 1.5 miles, turn N onto Portal Place and then L on Marine Dr, continuing 0.5 mile to the road end. From the south turn off Hwy 20 onto Parker Rd, go 1 mile and turn N onto Portal Place as above.

Parking: 10-15 ⛱🚶🏊🅿

Adjoining public tideland: 1.6 miles west to Captain Coupe Park, 0.9 mile east

Magnificent views of Mt. Baker and Oak Harbor await the visitor to Long Point. Great blue herons and eagles can be seen feeding at low tide. Butter clams, little necks, horse clams and cockles are common beneath the surface of this sandy beach. Before digging clams here, as at all sites, be sure to check with the Biotoxin Hotline, Wash. Dept. of Health, and Island County Health Dept. for shellfish closures. Clam diggers should be sure to observe limits and fill in the clam holes. For more information see p. 118.

Race Week viewed from Long Point

Ebey's Prairie agriculture

Hiking trails, overlooks, county roads and numerous public access points give visitors captivating views of the rich farm fields of Ebey's Prairie on central Whidbey. While most of this land is privately owned, it is preserved for future generations as agricultural land within the 17,400-acre Ebey's Landing National Historical Reserve. Glacial ice left three large natural prairies behind when it receded. The prairies were once lake beds. Today about a third of these lands are planted in squash, grains, forage and seed crops.

Fields of Ebey's Prairie with Mt. Baker in the background

Site 28 — EBEY'S LANDING
Lat/Long: N 48° 11.542, W 122° 43.858

Directions: From Hwy 20 north of the traffic light at Coupeville, turn S onto Terry Rd, keep straight ahead on Ebey Rd and proceed to the beach.

Parking: 10+

Adjoining public tideland: West 2 miles to Fort Ebey State Park and southeast 2 miles to Fort Casey State Park.

Ebey's Landing is part of Ebey's Landing National Historical Reserve and provides excellent exploration of bluffs and beaches. From the Landing, walkable beaches stretch far to the north. Before leaving on a long beach hike, check your tide tables. Tides in the Pacific Northwest are described as being semidiurnal mixed tides, two high tides and two low tides of mixed heights in a 24-hour time period. An extremely high tide, coupled with wind-driven waters, can create a very hazardous situation leaving the beachcomber stranded with no upland access.

A trail ascends stairs and climbs the bluff, curving along the top with commanding views of the beach below, Admiralty Inlet, the Olympic Mountains and both Mt. Rainier and Mt. Baker. The plant community on this bluff is one of the few remaining examples of a natural, coastal prairie ecosystem. Few comparable areas remain in our state, most having been lost in the last 150 years to farming and bluff-top homes. The trail follows the bluff about 1¾ miles before descending steeply to the beach at the west end of Perego's Lagoon, a brackish, saltwater wetland located between beach and bluff. The round trip is about 3½ miles.

Ebey's Landing can also be reached on foot from Cemetery Road. Turn W off Hwy 20 onto Sherman Rd and continue straight on Cemetery Rd. Park on the L at the Prairie Overlook opposite the far end of the cemetery. Ebey's Prairie Trail starts here and skirts private land to reach Ebey's Bluff. The historic Sunnyside Cemetery is also interesting to explore.

Ebey's Landing from the bluff trail

We're choking on plastic

Did you know we have a 500-square-mile "floating garbage patch" in the north Pacific? It's trapped there by currents. Researchers have found six pounds of plastic floating for every pound of zooplankton. Plastic is made of long molecules not found in nature and does not biodegrade. It just breaks apart into smaller and smaller pieces, becoming part of the plankton and entering the bodies of filter-feeding shellfish, plankton-eating birds, fish and larger organisms, working its way up the food chain. Some plastic is discarded at sea, but most washes or blows from the land. What can we do? Pick up plastic on the beach. Use less plastic. Reuse when possible. Recycle. Find alternatives.

Site 29   FORT CASEY STATE PARK
Lat/Long: N 48° 09.826, W 122° 40.695

Directions: Located next to Keystone Harbor. From the north: From Hwy 20 at Coupeville turn S onto Main St, which becomes Engle Rd. Travel 3.5 miles to park entrance on S side, after Camp Casey and before the Keystone Ferry terminal. From the south: Go 5 miles N of Greenbank on Hwy 525 to the intersection with Race Rd. Turn W onto Hwy 20 toward the Keystone Ferry landing. After 1.75 miles the highway makes a 90° turn S, then turns 90° W to parallel the south shore of Crockett Lake. The park entrance is on the L 0.25 mile past the ferry terminal.

The park provides excellent access to beaches and amenities. For information contact the state park (360-678-4519) or go to **www.parks.wa.gov**.

Of all the ships to sail past Whidbey Island's Admiralty Head into Puget Sound in the last three centuries, none left a greater legacy than the HMS Discovery in 1792, under the command of Captain George Vancouver. Vancouver named the high bluff Admiralty Head. The commanding site soon had a lighthouse and then a coastal artillery post, Fort Casey, which still enthralls visitors with its historic guns and spectacular vista over Admiralty Inlet. Two miles of shoreline beach are available for walking, and a wide parade field atop the windblown bluff is popular for kite flying.

Admiralty Head Lighthouse, built in 1901 to replace the original wooden structure, is a historic landmark and interpretive center, open seasonally. The lighthouse is kept open to the public under a cooperative agreement between WSU Extension and Washington State Parks. It is headquarters of the Island County WSU Extension environmental programs–Beach Watchers, Keepers of Admiralty Head Lighthouse, and Waste Wise. A trail behind the lighthouse leads through a compost demonstration site. (Trail map p. 143)

Site 30   KEYSTONE JETTY (Fort Casey State Park)
Lat/Long: N 48° 09.493, W 122° 40.257

Directions: Located alongside the Keystone Ferry landing, S of Coupeville. Follow directions to Site 29, continuing east to the parking area and boat launch on the east shore of the ferry harbor.

Parking: 50+

Adjoining public tideland: Jetty and Park only.

The constructed Keystone Jetty has interrupted the natural longshore movement of sediment. This structure causes beach accretion (addition) on the updrift side (ferry channel) and beach erosion on the downdrift side. The jetty, part of the protected Keystone Conservation Area, is a popular dive site and displays a vast collection of sea anemones making a living among the rocks. Use caution, especially when venturing out on the jetty during wet weather or heavy wave action.

Fort Casey Underwater State Park—a hidden treasure

Just out of sight in the dark waters next to 250-foot Keystone Jetty at Fort Casey is a wonderland of marine plants and animals, brilliantly colorful and fabulously diverse. Scuba divers from across Washington, British Columbia and the Northwest travel here to find and photograph 50-year-old rockfish, mature ling cod as big as children, giant Pacific octopus, wolf eels, buffalo sculpin, kelp greenling, great cabezon and surf perch. The cold waters and swift currents around Keystone Jetty ensure a rich food supply for plants and animals, which find shelter in a habitat ranging from sand and cobble to large boulders. Adding to the rich display are large plumose anemones, bull kelp and eelgrass, and countless varieties of sea cucumbers, crabs, sea stars, barnacles and tube worms. The anemone garden covers thousands of square feet.

Fort Casey Underwater State Park was established by the Washington State Parks & Recreation Commission in the early 1970s as part of a system of underwater parks to provide high-quality dive sites for recreation and to preserve Washington's marine resources. Keystone Conservation Area is a Marine Protected Area of the Washington Department of Fish & Wildlife. It lies entirely inside the boundaries of the underwater park and is closed to all consumptive recreational activities.

Because of the powerful currents, nearby fishing and boating activity, ferry crossing and other hazards, divers are strongly advised to ask for a thorough safety briefing about this area before setting out. Experienced divers who know this site may be located by inquiring at dive shops in Oak Harbor or Anacortes.

© Jim Ramaglia

Grunt sculpin at Keystone

Site 31 — KEYSTONE SPIT (Fort Casey State Park)

Lat/Long: N 48° 09.795, W 122° 39.489 (west entrance)
N 48° 09.877, W 122° 38.831 (east entrance)

Directions: Follow directions for Ft. Casey State Park and continue east of the ferry dock past the private residences. Vehicles may enter parking areas at two points along the spit, one located 0.6 mile E of the ferry slip, the other 1.1 miles E of the ferry slip, shortly E of milepost 14. (From the south, the easternmost Keystone Spit parking entry is 0.5 mile W of Site 32.)

Parking: 50+ 🛬🏕🛶🏌

Adjoining public tideland: 1.5 miles. Bordered by the homes just east of the Jetty and by Keystone Rd.

Keystone Spit, part of Fort Casey State Park, is a 2-mile stretch of land separating Admiralty Inlet and Crockett Lake. Along the tidelands is an enormous amount of driftwood and logs blown up onto the backshore by prevailing winds. Crockett Lake is a 700-acre mixture of salt and fresh water marshes, mudflats, open water and grasslands, providing rich feeding for a variety of birdlife. It is designated as an Important Bird Area for Washington state because large numbers of shorebirds use it as a stopover during their northbound (April-May) and southbound (early July-October) migrations. Nine species of ducks and 17 species of shorebirds have been recorded here. These draw raptors including northern harriers, peregrine falcons, merlins, short-eared owls and bald eagles. The lake also provides rich foraging for great blue herons during breeding season. An ADA-friendly observation platform for bird watching can be found on the south side of the highway immediately south of milepost 14, at the west end of the eastern vehicle access point (see below).

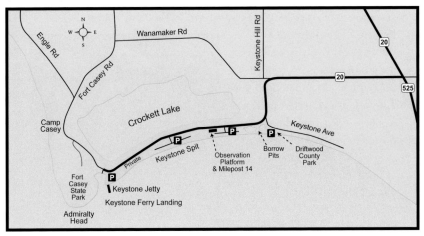

Keystone Spit pullouts and observation platform.

Bird observation platform at Keystone Spit

Five Island County sites listed as essential for birds

*The Important Bird Areas (IBA) program is a worldwide effort to iden-
tify key places of importance for maintaining healthy bird populations. In
2001 Audubon Washington designated 53 IBAs in Washington as "sites
most essential for long-term conservation of birds." The list includes five
in Island County–Crescent Harbor Marshes, Penn Cove, Crockett Lake,
Deer Lagoon and Port Susan.*

*Three of these sites, Penn Cove, Crockett Lake and Deer Lagoon,
were declared Habitats of Local Importance (HOLI) by Island County
government in August 2000 (Ordinance C-78-00), as part of the
county's Critical Areas Ordi-
nance. Other HOLIs listed in
the ordinance are Swan Lake
(a.k.a Bos Lake, a.k.a. Swantown
Lake), Hastie Lake, Whidbey
Island Game Farm (now Au
Sable Environmental Institute),
Newman Road Ponds (now part
of Earth Sanctuary), Useless Bay
and Cultus Bay Flats.*

Great blue heron

© Craig Johnson

DRIFTWOOD BEACH PARK
Lat/Long: N 48° 09.837, W 122° 38.232

Directions: From the south: Go 5 miles N of Greenbank on Hwy 525 to the intersection with Race Rd. Turn W onto Hwy 20 (Wanamaker Rd) toward the Keystone Ferry landing. After 1.75 miles the road makes a 90° turn S. In another 0.25mile, where Keystone Rd turns 90° W between the spit and Crockett Lake, go straight ahead into park at road end. From the north: Follow directions for Site 29. Continue E past ferry 2 miles. When highway turns 90° L, instead turn R into park.

Parking: 20

Adjoining public tideland: In front of park and 1.5 miles west along Keystone Spit.

The shore of this aptly-named ¾ acre park at the east end of Keystone Spit is piled thickly with driftwood, a reminder that this area is also a catch-point for drifting marine debris. In season it is a popular fishing site. Ducks are often seen in the two gravel borrow pits west of the parking lot. The park offers a view of the snowy peaks of the Olympic mountains and the busy shipping lanes between Whidbey Island and Fort Flagler. At lower tides, 1½ miles of beach walking is available along Keystone Spit to the west.

Driftwood Beach Park

LWD–you can't miss it

That tangle of sun-bleached logs pushed far onto the backshore by extreme tides and storms is what scientists call LWD–large woody debris. While it may look like a mess, it is actually a sophisticated shock absorber and much more. Most of those logs started out as trees along riverbanks or bluffs. These trees eventually became undercut and fell into the water. They floated to their present location and became knit together in a complex web that absorbs wave energy and helps hold soils, thereby reducing erosion of the shore. On the backshore they function to trap and release organic material, moisture and nutrients to help sustain plant life. These logs also provide resting and roosting spots for a variety of birds and other wildlife, and places for aquatic invertebrates to attach themselves.

Tempting as it may be to take home some driftwood from the beach, laws prohibit its removal in many jurisdictions. And it makes sense to leave it in place. Woody debris in general helps stabilize shorelines, and even small pieces provide useful shelter and habitat for beach-dwelling creatures. Driftwood removal is prohibited at Island County public recreational areas under section 17.05.190 of the shoreline use regulations, and at all state parks.

Site 33 LEDGEWOOD BEACH ACCESS (Driftwood Way)
Lat/Long: N 48° 08.586, W 122° 36.260

Directions: Turn W off Hwy 525 onto Ledgewood Beach Rd. At T intersection turn N onto Fircrest Ave for 0.5 mile, then W onto Seaward Way. Wind downhill to make sharp R hairpin turn onto Driftwood Way and follow it N 600 feet to parking area on L. Beach is accessed by a short set of stairs.
Parking: 5-6, **Amenities:** None, **Special uses:** 🚣 🚶
Adjoining public tideland: North 1 mile, south 1.5 miles.

No beach at high tide. Beach and coastline stability depend on the capability of coastal features to resist changes by geological, environmental or man-made events. Ledgewood Beach shows evidence of stability failure in all three. Excessive rains followed by a cold freeze caused the uplands to slough and slide in December of 1990, damaging two homes north of the parking lot. Another slide occurred in January 1997. Shoreline wave action has continued to erode the beach and bluffs. Bulkheads, which have fallen into the surf, and bluffs show evidence of continued recession. This beach can be very dangerous ¼ mile north of the beach access due to serious calving (large chunks of land falling) off the bluff. It is safest when in this area to always walk near the water's edge.

Site 34	HIDDEN BEACH (Crane's Landing Drive)
	Lat/Long: N 48° 07.727, W 122° 33.789

Directions: From Greenbank turn E off of Hwy 525 onto North Bluff Rd. In 2.25 miles turn E onto Neon Lane for a short block, then N on Crane's Landing Drive. Wind downhill to sea level. At bottom, turn N to the access at road end. To S is private community club. *Note: At time of printing, this access was closed to cars due to erosion of roadway and parking area during winter storms in 2006. It is still accessible by bicycle or on foot.*

Parking: Closed at time of printing ⛵🚶

Adjoining public tideland: 730 feet to north only, along isolated cobble beach with overhanging trees. Private to south.

Birds of the bluffs

The shores of Island County include miles of bluffs. In sections bare of vegetation you may have noticed round or oval holes, the nests of three bird species: belted kingfishers, rough-winged swallows and pigeon guillemots.

Kingfishers hover and dive

While walking the beach you may hear the reverberating rattle-like call of a belted kingfisher. It can be observed hovering over the water (an osprey does this also) looking for prey. The belted kingfisher is blue and white, with a white ring around its neck, a slate blue breast band and a shaggy crest on the back of its head. The female sports an additional rust-red belly band—a rare case among birds where the female of the species is more colorful than the male. If you see a kingfisher flying overhead, watch its wings beat a Morse-code pattern with flashing white wing patches.

Stocky and short-legged, this bird's power is in its large head and sharp bill. The king of fishers hovers over water and then dives headfirst to catch prey in its bill. Emerging from the water, the bird flies back to a perch. There it juggles the meal—usually a fish or aquatic invertebrate—into position and gulps it down.

In spring belted kingfishers dig nesting burrows in sandy bluffs. They use their front claws—with two forward-pointing toes fused together for added strength—and their strong bills to dig out holes. The burrows typically reach three to six feet into the bank. But some nesting holes can extend 15 feet into a sandy bank.

Swallows hunt in the air

The northern rough-winged swallow is an aerial artist. Its diet is 100% insects, which it usually catches in flight but occasionally plucks from the

*ground. Pale brown above and white below with a dingy brown breast,
these 5½-inch birds nest in a burrow or cavity. They use deserted
kingfisher burrows, rodent holes and ready-made niches in bridges,
wharves, culverts and other structures.*

Pigeon guillemots swim in groups

*In spring and summer you may spot groups of velvety-black seabirds with
white wing patches and bright red feet swimming near shore emitting
high-pitched, piping whistles and trilled songs. This is the pigeon guillemot, the only species in the alcid family (which includes puffins, murres
and auklets) that nests on Whidbey and Camano islands. They nest in
loose colonies in burrows or on ledges. Look for their holes in sandy
bluffs, often among the roots of bluff-top vegetation. Watch for their syn-
chronized courtship flights as pairs rocket over the water, turning as one.
In July and August the parents are busy carrying single fish to their one or
two chicks in the burrow.*

*Volunteers from Whidbey Audubon Society, working with the Island
County Marine Resources Committee, have begun surveying pigeon
guillemot colonies on Whidbey Island. In 2005 observers visited colonies
211 times, identified 153 nesting burrows and counted nearly 800 pigeon
guillemots. Activities recorded include pair interaction, visiting burrows,
catching fish and bringing food to the burrows.*

*Watch for these fascinating birds the next time you walk the beach
under our bluffs. To help this species maintain a viable population detour
around the birds if they are resting on the beach, walk quickly past their
colonies and keep your dog on a leash. This species is declining dramati-
cally in some areas and is now a species of concern.*

© Celia Bartram

Pigeon guillemot

Site 35 **LAGOON POINT NORTH** (Westcliff Drive)
Lat/Long: N 48° 04.963, W 122° 36.616

Directions: From the north: Turn W off Hwy 525 onto Smugglers Cove Rd (0.7 mile N of Greenbank). In 2.7 miles, turn R onto Westcliff Dr. At bottom of hill drive straight toward shore into gravel parking area. Signs mark private property to either side of the beach. From the south: Just N of Freeland turn W onto Bush Point Rd, which becomes Smugglers Cove Rd. In 6.6 miles turn L onto Westcliff Dr and follow directions above.

Parking: 10

Adjoining public tideland: North 160 feet, south 274 feet, below line of ordinary high tide.

This is a very popular salmon fishing beach. Lagoon Point offers views of the Olympic mountains, Port Townsend and a very active shipping lane.

Lagoon Point North

Whidbey's west side—paradise for shore fishers

One look at the map tells the story. Whidbey Island sits at the entrance to Puget Sound. Nearly every salmon, steelhead and sea-run cutthroat trout that migrates to the ocean and back from Puget Sound rivers will swim past Whidbey Island on the way.

Many of the returning southbound fish hug the shore to feast on the teeming forage fish that lay their eggs on Whidbey Island's nearshore eelgrass and healthy beaches. As a result, many anglers consider Whidbey Island's entire west side the state's number one bet for shore fishing.

Anglers enjoy year-round opportunities to fish miles of uncrowded public shoreline in the island's many parks and other public access areas. They look for rocky or gravelly shoreline and cast lures or bait with traditional salmon rods, fly gear or spinning reels.

Fly fishers typically are seeking the feisty sea-run cutthroat trout, which run 13 to 20 inches and come as close to shore as a few feet of the water's edge. Cutthroat migrate back to Puget Sound's larger rivers in the fall and, when caught in saltwater, must be released alive.

For silver salmon, pink salmon (also called humpies) and winter steelhead, shore anglers favor traditional spinning or salmon gear. Flies may be used but most anglers use bait such as plug-cut herring or Buzz Bombs, weighted jigs or a local favorite called the Bush Point rig. Salmon and steelhead typically will be found in four to six feet of water, so anglers will cast out about 40 feet. Pinks run every other year. Chinook salmon are caught incidentally, but are a protected species and must be released alive.

Top saltwater shore fishing areas on Whidbey Island include North Beach and West Beach in Deception Pass State Park, Keystone Spit near Fort Casey, Lagoon Point, Bush Point and Possession Point...and much of the shoreline in between!

Before planning any fishing trip, anglers should make sure they are properly licensed and carefully consult the official Sport Fishing Rules for Washington, published by the Washington Department of Fish & Wildlife, available at many hardware stores and other outlets where fishing tackle is sold. This publication provides detailed information on seasons, limits and other rules.

Site 36 LAGOON POINT SOUTH (Salmon Street)
Lat/Long: N 48° 04.315, W 122° 36.786

Directions: Follow Site 35 directions, turning off Smugglers Cove Rd onto Westcliff Dr. Turn L onto Lagoon View Dr, then R onto Salmon St. At end of Salmon St continue straight across intersection into access.

Parking: 2-3 ⚓ 🐟

Adjoining public tideland: 30 feet only. Please respect privately owned beach to either side.

This limited beach access is one of the better salmon and steelhead fishing sites in Island County. If you are not into fishing but are into waves, this beach is a great place to observe and ponder while enjoying a panoramic view of the Olympic mountain range.

Lagoon Point South

Site 37 SOUTH WHIDBEY STATE PARK
Lat/Long: N 48° 03.442, W 122° 35.566

Directions: From the north: Turn W off Hwy 525 onto Smugglers Cove Rd. Proceed 4 miles to park entrance on R (west) side of Smugglers Cove Rd. From the south: Just N of Freeland turn W onto Bush Point Rd, which becomes Smugglers Cove Rd. The park entrance is on L in 5 miles. The park provides most amenities. For information contact the state park (360-321-4559) or go to **www.parks.wa.gov**.

One of Island County's smaller state parks, South Whidbey offers over 50 attractive campsites nestled among forest undergrowth, picnic areas and barbecue pits, nearly a mile feet of secluded beach and an extensive hiking trail through the Classic U Forest, one of the best stands of old growth douglas firs and red cedars still remaining in Island County. This forest trail is east of Smugglers Cove Rd. Throughout spring and summer, blooming wildflowers and shrubs add color to the park and produce salmonberries, huckleberries and black-cap raspberries. From a kiosk in the paved parking area a ½ mile trail descends the 300-foot slope to the beach, with benches for resting on the trip back up. At lower tides visitors can enjoy clamming, crabbing, fishing and miles of beach walking. Avoid the beach at high tide when water reaches the foot of the bluff. (Trail map p. 145)

Orcas—our intelligent, sensitive marine neighbors

Few creatures inspire more outright awe than orcas or killer whales. These magnificent mammals are gifted with high intelligence, 50-year lifespans, complex communication and close family structure. They live, eat, relax and travel in groups, having much in common with their dominant terrestrial neighbor—human kind. Puget Sound's orcas live in family units called pods led by the eldest female. In the waters of Whidbey and Camano islands most orcas sighted from late fall through mid winter belong to the three pods of the Southern Resident population, J, K and L pods. This group communicates with calls completely different from the calls of other groups, even those found in the same waters, and probably has lived in Puget Sound since the glaciers retreated more than 10,000 years ago. The population has ranged in recent decades from about 80 to 100. In 2005, with fewer than 90 individuals remaining, the Southern Residents were federally listed as endangered. Unlike some other orca populations, the Southern Residents rely heavily on Chinook salmon for their diet. Declining salmon populations and increasing pollution are believed to be major contributors to the stress on the Southern Residents.

Site 38	BUSH POINT BOAT LAUNCH
	Lat/Long: N 48° 02.017, W 122° 36.179

Directions: From Hwy 525 just N of Freeland, turn W onto Bush Point Rd (becomes Smugglers Cove Rd) for 2.7 miles, fork L onto Scurlock Rd 0.75 mile, then L onto Spyglass Dr. Public access and boat launch are on R at bottom of hill. Continue L around the corner to large paved parking lot.
Parking: 12 car-only, 12+ vehicles with trailers

A new boat ramp provides the best deep-water access on the west side of south Whidbey. This site is managed by the Port of South Whidbey. The public access includes about 15 feet either side of boat launch. No stopping is allowed on the beach in front of the private houses either side of the access, but you can walk 400 feet N along the tideline past the houses to reach a long public beach popular for fishing or beach walking at the foot of the bluff. There is an expansive view west along Admiralty Inlet between the Olympic Peninsula and Whidbey Island. Whales are sometimes sighted from here.

© Dan Pedersen

Public beach north of Bush Point Boat Launch

Site 39 — BUSH POINT - SANDPIPER RD
Lat/Long: N 48° 01.942, W 122° 36.320

Directions: Follow Site 38 directions onto Spyglass Dr. At bottom of hill follow road to L, and at T intersection turn R onto Sandpiper Rd to road end.

Parking: 2-4

Adjoining public tideland: 45 feet. Do not access areas to south and north as these are privately owned beaches and tidelands. The beach and tidelands fronting on the lighthouse are also privately owned by homeowners and not available for access.

This limited-access site has been used for years as a salmon fishing beach.

Septic systems impact oysters, clams, mussels

As in rural areas everywhere, most sewage in Island County is treated on site, in household septic systems and drainfields. When these systems are overwhelmed or poorly maintained, bacteria can make their way into marine waters and contaminate shellfish beds and beaches, making shellfish unsafe to eat. It is a huge problem—in 2006 some 40 percent of Washington's shellfish beds were closed to harvest or restricted because of fecal contamination from septic systems. Homeowners can help greatly by following some preventive practices: 1) Having septic tanks pumped about every three years to remove solids, 2) Minimizing household water use through conservation to avoid taxing the capacity of their system, 3) Keeping grease, cigarettes, chemicals and other microbe-killing materials out of their septic systems, and 4) Keeping root-producing vegetation and heavy objects off their drainfields, to avoid damage to the system. (Contact Island County Health Department for more information.)

Site 40
MUTINY BAY VISTA (Shore Meadows Rd)
Lat/Long: N 48° 00.530, W 122° 34.311

Directions: Turn W off Hwy 525 onto Bush Point Rd. Travel 1.2 miles and turn S onto Shore Meadows Rd. Public access is at road end by the condominiums; parallel park on N side. A sidewalk leads SE downhill to the beach access.
Parking: 7
Adjoining public tideland: 295 feet, west from where the path reaches the beach to the tideland below the bluff in front the parking area. The sidewalk and access were provided to the public as a condition of the condominium development. Please respect the privacy of those living in the condominiums.

This small beach is typical of many westside Whidbey Island beaches in that it is primarily sandy and provides great views of the Olympic mountains. It's a long distance to the water with a hand-carry boat.

Site 41
FREELAND PARK
Lat/Long: N 48° 00.917, W 122° 31.840

Directions: Located in Freeland at the head of Holmes Harbor. From the north: From Hwy 525 turn N onto Honeymoon Bay Rd, then immediately E onto Shoreview Dr 0.7 mile, up hill past Freeland Hall and down to park. Boat launch and park are marked with signs. From the south: Turn N at traffic light onto Main St, then L at stop sign onto E Harbor Rd. Fork L downhill on Stewart Dr, continue 0.3 mi. to park.

Parking: 30+ 🍴🚻⛲🗑️🏠🛶🚤⛴️🚶🏕️

Adjoining public tideland: 720 feet of shoreline east of dock, 1,300 feet to west.

This park, owned by the Port of South Whidbey and managed by Island County Parks Dept., has a public moorage dock for day use. The tideflat slope is gradual; be cautious launching at mid to low tides to avoid being marooned in the mud. When the tide is low, you can see patches of eelgrass growing in the soft sandy mud, characteristic of the substrate at the heads of bays. As well as fish, other organisms benefit by living with the eelgrass including sponges, bryozoans, small worms and tunicates. In Holmes Harbor, herring use the eelgrass for reproduction by attaching their eggs to the long eelgrass blades. The park extends up the hill to the west with a picnic shelter and a woodland trail and includes Freeland Hall, built in 1907 and available for rental from Island County.

Forage fish 'fuel' the marine food web

*Three tiny fish—**surf smelt, sand lance** and **herring**—prowl the waters of Camano and Whidbey islands in vast numbers, laying a banquet for salmon, seabirds and marine mammals. They are Puget Sound's pre-eminent forage fish—fish that transfer energy between primary and secondary producers, such as plankton, to top predators such as seabirds and larger fish, forming a vital link in the marine food chain.*

For centuries, forage fish have been an important subsistence food for tribal cultures and continue to be harvested both recreationally and commercially. Herring are a favorite bait for recreational salmon fishing.

Beach walkers sometimes observe shifting clouds of these little fish darting in the shallows just beyond the water's edge, or spot them from above while looking down from over-water piers such as Coupeville Wharf.

Pacific sand lance and surf smelt lay their eggs on protected sandy gravel beaches of Camano and Whidbey islands near the high tide line at certain times of year. Pacific herring spawn directly on the lush vegetation in the many intertidal eelgrass beds of Camano and Whidbey. These same eelgrass beds offer refuge and shelter to juvenile salmon.

Forage-fish 'fuel' the marine food web (cont.)

Because forage fish are so important to salmon and other marine life, Island County Marine Resources Committee recently mapped every beach on Camano and Whidbey islands where forage fish are known to spawn, as a step toward preserving healthy habitat. Greater understanding of these fish and the habitat they require will aid efforts to restore salmon populations.

Sand lance and surf smelt benefit from beaches with low wave energy where overhanging trees shade the upper shore from midday sun, helping keep their eggs cooler. They also benefit from beaches relatively free of man-made structures, which can concentrate wave energy that scours away spawning gravels. All forage fish and juvenile salmon benefit from healthy eelgrass beds.

Site 42   MUTINY BAY BOAT LAUNCH (Robinson Road)
Lat/Long: N 47° 59.599, W 122° 32.458

Directions: From the Hwy 525 traffic light at Freeland turn S onto Fish Rd. Follow for 1 mile to T intersection and turn L onto Mutiny Bay Rd. After 0.3 mile, turn R onto Robinson Rd to beach access straight ahead. Please use the large parking area provided on the north side of Robinson Rd 150 feet before beach.

Parking: 15+

Adjoining public tideland: 60 feet only at the boat ramp.

Mutiny Bay Boat Launch

This boat launch on a shallow, sandy bay is only usable for shallow-draft boats at optimal tides. The ramp frequently sands in, requiring a lot of maintenance. The launch at Bush Point is a better alternative for most watercraft, especially larger boats. Co-owned by Island County and the Port of South Whidbey, this access is managed by Island County Parks.

Site 43 — MUTINY BAY SHORES (Limpet Lane)
Lat/Long: N 47° 58.606, W 122° 33.067

Directions: From the Hwy 525 traffic light at Freeland turn S onto Fish Rd. Follow for 1 mile to T intersection and turn L onto Mutiny Bay Rd. After 0.6 mile turn R onto Wahl Rd. At Ebb Tide Lane turn R, then L onto Limpet Lane. From Mutiny Bay Rd to the access is 3 miles.

Parking: 1-2

Adjoining public tideland: 950 feet to the NE.

Mutiny Bay Shores is a small public beach with close-up views of passing ships. The lower beach is mostly small, clean cobble transitioning to sand in the upper areas.

Glacial erratics

Twenty-thousand years ago, Whidbey and Camano islands were covered by ice nearly a mile deep. This was the Puget Lobe of the Vashon Glacier, which flowed south from British Columbia. The direction in which the glaciers flowed is reflected by the north-south orientation of most hills and valleys on Whidbey and Camano islands, plainly visible on detailed elevation maps (see map on p. 130). As the ice advanced it carved large rocks from mountains and hills in the north and carried them south to where it melted and dropped this odd cargo randomly. Many of these out-of-place "glacial erratics" now sit in plain view on the fields and beaches of Whidbey and Camano islands. They range from wheelbarrow-size to house-size. When located in the intertidal zone, these huge boulders provide a window into the diversity of sedentary marine life. The lower flanks of erratics house a mosaic of colorful, minute animal colonies known as bryozoans, along with pink coralline algae, calcareous tube worms, limpets, chitons, and giant barnacles.

Site 44 | DOUBLE BLUFF BEACH
Lat/Long: N 47° 58.910, W 122° 30.850

Directions: Turn S off Hwy 525 (9 miles from Clinton) onto Double Bluff Rd. Follow 2 miles to parking lot at road end.

Parking: 24. Do not block driveway at access.

Adjoining public tideland: 2 miles to west, none to east.

The two mile long sandy beach is popular for family picnics and beach walking. An off-leash area for dogs begins beyond the windsock. Please pay attention to off-leash guidelines and rules, and clean up after your dog. A rinse station is provided near the parking lot. At low tide look for giant moon snails shoveling through the sand in search of clams to feast on. The sandy beach sediments come from the erosion of tall bluffs west of the access. Eroding bluffs are not a safe place to play. Keep off the bluffs. Also be aware that at higher tides there is no return to the public access when water reaches the foot of the bluff. High bluffs like these provide nesting burrows for pigeon guillemots, belted kingfishers and rough-winged swallows (box, p. 55).

Double Bluff Beach

Feeder bluffs provide spawning gravels

Glacially carved bluffs dominate large stretches of shoreline on Whidbey and Camano islands. The erosion and redistribution of material from these bluffs over time by wave and wind action are natural processes that help maintain healthy beaches and habitat for marine life. These bluffs continuously replenish beaches with sand and gravel of the ideal size and consistency for use by forage fish to lay their eggs. Island County's abundant forage fish are a key part of the food chain that sustains salmon and other marine life. Gravel erodes from the bluff and falls to the beach. It is distributed along the shoreline by littoral drift—the current that prevails on a specific segment of beach, determined by the angle at which waves routinely strike the shoreline at that point. Then, forage fish spawn in this gravel. During 2004-05, Island County Marine Resources Committee engaged geologists to identify and map all the feeder bluffs and drift cells on the county's 212 miles of shoreline. This is the most complete study of its kind ever done. It will help shoreline planners and property owners better understand and conserve these essential sources of the sediment that maintains our beaches.

<table>
<tr><td>**Site 45**</td><td>DEER LAGOON
Lat/Long: N 47° 59.688, W 122° 30.428</td></tr>
</table>

Directions: Located E of Double Bluff Rd, the lagoon is owned by Island County, but at time of writing, there is no good shore access. You can park on the wide E shoulder of Double Bluff Rd 0.5 mile from road's end and drag a canoe to the lagoon with hip waders, or watch birds from the road verge.

Parking: 1-2 ⚓🛶

The salt marsh is a highly productive tideland ecosystem with salt tolerant grasses and sedges. Bird watchers will find a variety of water and land birds that use Deer Lagoon for feeding and nesting. Deer Lagoon is surrounded by private land. Please respect private property.

<table>
<tr><td>**Site 46**</td><td>SUNLIGHT BEACH ACCESS
Lat/Long: N 47° 59.456, W 122° 28.924</td></tr>
</table>

Directions: From Hwy 525, turn S onto Bayview Rd. After a mile turn R onto Sunlight Beach Rd, driving slowly through this densely packed waterfront community. The county owned access is located in 0.9 mile, between the house at 2440 E. Sunlight Beach Rd and the house at 2436 E. Sunlight Beach Rd. The public access extends to both sides of the street, to a lagoon on the N and Useless Bay on the S. Parking is on the left (southside) access. Do not park on Sunlight Beach Rd or in front of any homes.

Parking: 2 ⚓🚶🛶

Adjoining public tideland: None to east, west around to Deer Lagoon.

The mud of the shallow lagoon limits the north side to primarily a view access. The more usable access is the south side sandy beach on Useless Bay. Be cautioned that when the tide goes down the water goes out a very long way. Know your tides before launching any boats so you don't become marooned. At low tides the bay becomes a vast expanse of sand flats stretching north to Double Bluff. Here feeding birds dig for burrowing invertebrates. Bird watch-

ers may want to walk a couple hundred feet back along the road to a public path on the left, just before 2467 E. Sunlight Beach Rd., which leads up onto the dike. Open water on both sides of the dike attracts a variety of birds.

Dowitchers

Sunlight Beach Access

Site 47   LONE LAKE (fresh water)
Lat/Long: N 48° 01.423, W 122° 27.653

Directions: From Hwy 525, turn N at traffic light onto Bayview Rd. After 1.5 miles, turn W onto Andreason Rd to stop sign, then L on Lone Lake Rd. Continue straight as it becomes a single lane gravel road before ending at park with large open field and lake access.

Parking: 20

This small, fresh water lake is popular for fishing. Varied habitat attracts birds of water, marsh and forest edge. The access is owned by Wash. Dept. of Fish & Wildlife and managed by Island County Parks Dept.

Site 48   GOSS LAKE (fresh water)
Lat/Long: N 48° 02.357, W 122° 28.68

Directions: From Hwy 525, turn N at traffic light onto Bayview Rd. After 1.5 miles, turn W onto Andreason Rd to stop sign. Go N on Lone Lake Rd 0.5 mile, W onto Goss Lake Rd 0.5 mile, then S onto Traverse Rd. At T go R on Lakeside Dr. Park is on L in 0.1 mile.

Parking: 8

No petroleum-powered motors are allowed on Goss Lake. This small lakeside county park is surrounded by private homes. Please respect the quiet and privacy of neighbors.

Goss Lake

WSU Beach Watchers bring citizen science to the shore

Island County's beaches are teeming with life, but constantly changing with the ebb and flow of tides and human activity. Trends in intertidal life are a key indicator of the health of upland areas as well as marine waters. So every year since 1995 an army of volunteers from WSU Beach Watchers has diligently mapped the diversity and density of intertidal plants and animals at more than 30 shoreline sites ranging from quiet mudflats to wave-battered cobbled shorelines. It is challenging work, often on rocky and slippery terrain, but is building a priceless, quality-controlled database to help marine scientists understand what is changing over time. Beach profiling is a labor of love for these volunteers, who are adept at recognizing dozens of different plants and creatures, and who rigorously adhere to a field-tested monitoring protocol. They are the only group annually collecting and compiling such baseline information about Island County beaches.

Directions: Located in the City of Langley. Get to Langley from Hwy 525 by turning onto Bayview Rd, Maxwelton Rd, or Langley Rd. The waterfront park can be reached via Tom Hladkey Park at the intersection of First St and Anthes Ave or by stairs from the overlook on First St by the "Boy and His Dog" statue.

Parking: City streets 🎪 🏃 🏖 🐟 🚣 A public restroom is two blocks away, SE of the intersection of Second St and Anthes.

Adjoining public tideland: 1,000 feet

Enjoy the view of Saratoga Passage with the "Boy and His Dog" statue located by the stairs on First Street. From this vantage point you can see sedimentary features made by currents and shifting sands. These include rill marks produced by water draining from the beach, swash marks composed of debris stranded by receding waves, and ripples produced by tidal currents. Migrating gray whales feed on ghost shrimp in the intertidal area during spring, leaving bathtub-sized depressions in the sand. Seawall Park itself is a flat, grassy bank that runs above the shore between a concrete bulkhead and an embankment. Steps give access to the beach. Picnic tables provide views of boat traffic in Saratoga Passage and sometimes of passing whales. Across the channel are the bluffs at Camano Head.

Beach Watchers map intertidal life in front of the Langley Seawall.

Ghost shrimp–gray whales love 'em

If you've wondered what creates the little volcano-shaped mounds on beaches with a mixed sand and mud substrate, the answer is ghost shrimp (Neotrypaea californiensis). Beneath the surface, these four-inch crustaceans carve out U-shaped tunnels that may descend more than two feet into the muddy sand. Here they feed on detritus in the mud. Like out-of-town guests, an assortment of commensal species may move into the tunnel with the ghost shrimp. These include the arrow goby (Clevelandia ios), which is a small fish, tiny pea crabs, a species of scaleworm, and a small clam. Gray whales come into shallow Island County waters to scoop up bathtub-sized mouthfuls of muddy sand, then use their tongue and baleen to sift out a feast of ghost shrimp.

Site 50 LANGLEY BOAT HARBOR & FISHING PIER
Lat/Long: N 48° 02.304, W 122° 24.275

Directions: Located at the E end of downtown Langley off First St. Turn N onto Wharf St near the intersection of First and Second streets and follow signs down short hill and R to city dock and Phil Simon Park.

Parking: 10

Adjoining public tideland: 200 feet

The beach is composed of sand and gravel and supports eelgrass beds in some of the lower tide zones. An elevated fishing pier can be reached by the harbor access bridge. Sea stars, jellyfish, and crabs are visible from the dock. Look across Saratoga Passage to Camano Island and east to the Cascades. This site is popular with scuba divers.

Langley Boat Harbor, with Camano Island in the distance

Yes we have gulls, just no seagulls

Have you ever looked for "seagull" in the index of a birding guide? It is not listed. That is because these birds are more correctly called "gulls," with many species, some of which are found far from the sea.

The most common gull in the Puget Sound lowlands is the glaucous-winged gull ("glaucous" means gray). Glaucous-winged gulls have gray wings all the way down to and including their wing tips.

Through the year, 12 other species of gulls wander into our area. Summer and fall bring large numbers of Bonaparte gulls, mew gulls and ring-billed gulls, but still well over 70% of all the gulls you see following the ferryboats, scavenging for food or just standing around are glaucous-winged gulls.

© Craig Johnson

Glaucous-winged gull

| Site 51 | MAXWELTON NATURE PRESERVE & OUTDOOR CLASSROOM (fresh water) |

Lat/Long: N 47° 57.389, W 122° 26.234

Directions: From Hwy 525, turn S onto Maxwelton Rd and travel 3.5 miles to parking entrance on L, just before French Rd. A carvedlog salmon sculpture marks the site.

Parking: 7 🚶

This 6¾ acre preserve at 7015 S. Maxwelton Road, on Maxwelton Creek, offers a self-guided interpretive trail, wetland boardwalk and streamside viewing platforms. No dogs, please. The preserve sits in a forested wetland of water-loving plants and sponge-like soils, and is owned by South Whidbey School District. A fully equipped outdoor classroom, built with volunteer labor and community donations, is used to educate hundreds of local students each year and also for periodic classes for the community to learn about watersheds, habitat, and salmon. For more information contact Whidbey Watershed Stewards at 360-579-1272 or www.whidbeywatersheds.org.

Whidbey's largest watershed attracts determined salmon

Maxwelton Creek is one of only two salmon-bearing streams on Whidbey Island, the other being neighboring Glendale Creek. Maxwelton Creek supports coho (silver salmon) as well as sea-run cutthroat. The watershed extends north past the intermediate and high schools and south to Swede Hill Road. The creek and its tributaries, such as Quade Creek, drain the watershed through more than 12 miles of stream before reaching the outflow at Maxwelton Beach, opposite the pond, where it runs under the road through a culvert and a tide gate.

Maxwelton Creek's brown cola color comes from the infusion of tannins as water flows through peat bogs on its way to Useless Bay. At 7,834 acres, Maxwelton Watershed is the largest of 125 watersheds in the county. The soil holds water year-round, slowing floods during winter rains and seeping moisture during dry summers. Native plants such as sword fern, salal, huckleberry, oceanspray and Oregon grape help prevent erosion along stream banks.

In the 1990s, community volunteers came together to form the non-profit Maxwelton Salmon Adventure, which has since become Whidbey Watershed Stewards. They work with the community to promote watershed stewardship and with interested landowners to restore and protect habitat on their creekside properties.

Much more information about this watershed may be found in the book, "A Journey Through the Maxwelton Watershed, a Natural and Social History," published by Maxwelton Salmon Adventure in 2002. It is available from island bookstores and historical societies.

Site 52 **DAVE MACKIE PARK**
Lat/Long: N 47° 56.357, W 122° 26.670

Directions: From Hwy 525, turn S onto Maxwelton Rd and travel 5 miles to the Maxwelton Beach community. The shoreside county park is on the R, fields and large picnic shelter on L.

Parking: 50

Adjoining public tideland: 420 feet.

A popular family park with a ballfield, basketball hoop, play equipment, tables, benches, shelters, boat launch and sand beach. The site is co-owned by Island County and the Port of South Whidbey. The historic group picnic shelter with brick stove BBQ can be reserved by calling Island County Parks. The tidelands are long and shallow, so the ramp is useful only for launching smaller boats at mid to high tide. From fall to spring, many water birds feed in the bay between here and Double Bluff, including loons, grebes, ducks and gulls. Brant geese stop by to browse on eelgrass.

Dave Mackie Park

Maxwelton and the Chautauqua

For a few brief years in the early 1900s tiny Maxwelton made a big name for itself. Situated below a 200-acre estuary formed by Island County's largest creek and watershed, Maxwelton in 1910 hosted the first Northwest Chautauqua, attracting shiploads of summer visitors from throughout the Puget Sound region. The Chautauqua movement brought together social and religious interests, offering Bible study, recreation and lectures on history, art and science. Four Scottish immigrants had founded Maxwelton in 1905—brothers Theodore Seaman Mackie, Peter Howard Mackie, David Thomas Mackie and James Herbert Mackie. They promoted the Chautauqua by constructing an amphitheater to seat 4,000 and promising visitors a bathing beach with a quarter mile of clean white sand and ample tent sites. The Maxwelton Chautauqua ended in 1916 when heavy snows collapsed the amphitheater roof. Today, Maxwelton is a quiet beach community of seasonal and year-round homes. Visitors picnic or launch boats at Dave Mackie Park and walk the sandy beach. Every summer for a few brief hours, thousands of visitors still converge on Maxwelton for a community Fourth of July parade of several blocks that has become a Whidbey Island institution.

Site 53 — DEER LAKE (fresh water)
Lat/Long: N 47° 58.447, W 122° 22.824

Directions: From Clinton ferry dock go uphill on Hwy 525 and turn S by the Post Office onto Deer Lake Rd. In 1.2 miles turn N onto Lake Shore Dr. Take first L, Bucktail Lane, to the public beach. From the north, turn S onto Cultus Bay Rd, then L onto Deer Lake Rd to Lake Shore Dr.

Parking: 6

This is a small fresh water lake mostly surrounded by homes. An eroded concrete ramp may be used for launching small boats. Floats mark a swimming area off the sand and gravel beach. (No lifeguard.)

Site 54 — CLINTON BEACH & PIER
Lat/Long: N 47° 58.498, W 122° 21.048

Directions: Located at the Clinton Ferry Terminal on the W side of the ferry dock. Turn N at the traffic light just before the dock.

Parking: Public parking

Adjoining public tideland: 179 feet in front of the park

© Dan Pedersen

A living roof tops the new picnic shelter at Clinton Beach

Acquired by the Port of South Whidbey in 2004, this half-acre beachfront site is fully ADA accessible. The picnic shelter features a living roof and the viewing platform is made of recycled materials. Adjoining it along the north side of the ferry dock is a public fishing pier and, beyond it, a ramp to a short-term boat moorage dock (day use). A rinse station also is provided. The beach is sandy and eelgrass beds just offshore support a wide variety of life, including juvenile fish (box, p. 22). There is very limited short-term parking on site. Public parking is available at the Port's lot on Humphrey Rd, the state park-and-ride lot at Deer Lake Rd, and the pay lot by the SE corner of the ferry dock. Although it is possible to launch a kayak or canoe, traveling south from here is not recommended due to the ferry traffic.

Report stranded marine mammals

Seals, sea lions, whales, dolphins and porpoises sometimes turn up on Island County beaches dead or apparently stranded. Seal pups should be left alone (box B-29). Please report dead or stranded mammals to the Central Puget Sound Marine Mammal Stranding Network, (Whidbey) 360-678-3765 or 1-866-ORCANET, or (Camano) 360-387-8299. Members of the network are volunteers authorized and trained by the National Marine Fisheries Service to investigate and collect scientific data that becomes part of a national database to track the health of our local marine population, environment and the effects of pollution within the food web. To join the network, call 360-678-3765 or 1-866-ORCANET.

Site 55 | GLENDALE PARKING ACCESS
Lat/Long: N 47° 56.386, W 122° 21.459

Directions: From Hwy 525 uphill of the Clinton Ferry terminal, turn S onto Humphrey Rd. In 3 miles, at bottom of hill where road enters Glendale and Seaway Lane branches N, turn E to short gravel county access between two houses. This is the only public parking access in Glendale, and is 200 feet N of the intersection with Glendale Rd. Parking is limited, and *the tidelands in front of the access are private.* This site can be used for a vista stop or for parking while walking to Glendale Road to view the channel restoration.

Parking: 2-3

Adjoining public tideland: Public access is the 30-foot road width only to the Meander Line. Below this the tideland is in private ownership.

Historically, Glendale Creek is one of two salmon-bearing streams on Whidbey Island. During the mid-20th century, the creek was diverted into a concrete culvert to reduce flooding in the small Glendale community. Unfortunately the length and structure of the culvert prevented salmon from returning to spawn. Storms during the winter of 1996/1997 damaged Glendale Road and blew out the culvert, opening it to daylight. In the fall of 1997, after a 50-year absence, salmon returned to the lower reach of Glendale

Creek. The county set out to design repairs that would allow salmon passage. Shorter crossing culverts were built, and restoration in the lower channel included lowering the creek bed, adding native vegetation along both sides, and installing rocks and cedar log weirs to mimic natural creek flows. Upstream, a culvert crossing under Glendale Road was replaced. This eliminated a fish blockage and created fish-friendly access above Glendale Road. Today the creek supports small spawning populations of chum and coho salmon.

Site 56   POSSESSION POINT STATE PARK
Lat/Long: N 47° 54.450, W 122° 22.585

Directions: From Hwy 525, turn S at traffic light onto Cultus Bay Rd. After 4.5 miles turn L onto Possession Rd. Travel 2 miles and turn R onto Franklin Rd. Narrow parking area in 0.4 mile signals end of public road (no turning space for trailers). Walk down gravel drive to trail around lawn leading down steps to shore. Upland trails are in development.

Parking: 10   🅿 ⛲ 🥾 🛶 🚶

Adjoining public tideland: None to north, nearly a mile south around Possession Point.

Possession Point is located on the far south end of Whidbey Island. This 25-acre park offers scenic beach walking around the bluff to the south. Frequent slides continually reveal new geological stories. The park is administered by South Whidbey State Park (360-321-4559). The house is occupied by park staff; please respect their privacy.

Volunteers are building a steep, challenging trail to the highest point, about one mile each way from the parking area. It will lead to a dramatic overlook down Puget Sound toward Seattle.

Washington Water Trails campsite at Possession Point State Park

> ## Captain Vancouver was feeling possessive
>
> *"Possession" refers to Captain George Vancouver's claiming for the King the shores he had explored. The ceremony took place on the east shore of Possession Sound, the body of water between the southern part of Whidbey Island and the mainland, which forms the entrance to Port Susan. The Mukilteo-Clinton ferry crosses Possession Sound.*

Site 57 | POSSESSION BEACH WATERFRONT PARK
Lat/Long: N 47° 54.729, W 122° 22.562

Directions: Follow directions above to Possession Rd, and 50 feet past Franklin Rd turn R into entry road to park and boat launch.

Parking: 30+

Adjoining public tideland: 677 feet.

The day-use park and launch give access to one of the most superb sport fishing areas in Puget Sound. Anglers can catch their limits of lingcod during bottom fish openings. Several species of salmon run off the point during migration and are a prize during seasonal openings. Possession Point Bait releases 50,000 coho each year, sponsored by Stilly/Snohomish Fisheries Enhancement Group and Puget Sound Anglers. This park offers a fine view of the ferries plying back and forth between Clinton and Mukilteoand the busy boat traffic in Possession Sound. The Dorothy Cleveland Trail offers a 1½ mile round-trip walk uphill to an elevation of 390 feet.

Possession Beach Waterfront Park

Derelict gear keeps on killing

Out of sight and out-of-mind, a tragic waste occurs every day in Island County and Puget Sound. Salmon, shellfish, bottom fish, marine mammals, aquatic birds and other creatures fall victim to thousands of lost commercial fishing nets, crab pots, shrimp pots, discarded lines and recreational gear snagged on the sea floor. This debris also endangers divers, swimmers and boaters. Island County Marine Resources Committee and the Northwest Straits Commission are leading the push to raise awareness of the problem, encourage the public to report lost gear,

© Phyllis Kind

and physically retrieve it. Specially-trained dive crews have begun the long overdue work to recover this massive quantity of gear. To report the discovery of derelict gear, phone the statewide hotline: 1-800-477-6224 or complete the Washington Department of Fish & Wildlife online report form: www.wdfw. wa.gov/fish/derelict/derelict_gear.htm.

A derelict fishing net is hoisted from the waters off Keystone Spit, on west Whidbey Island. An experienced crew from Natural Resources Consultants cut the net free and removed it as part of a cleanup project for the Northwest Straits Commission and Island County Marine Resources Committee. The net had been snagged on pilings at this popular diving location for more than a year, posing a hazard to scuba divers and killing marine life and birds. Crabs and fish were entangled in it. The dock where it was snagged is a nesting site for pigeon guillemots and a roost for cormorants.

CAMANO ISLAND SITES

Sixteen miles long and from one to seven miles wide, Camano Island is tucked between Whidbey Island to the west and the mainland to the east. It is surrounded by the waters of Port Susan, Skagit Bay and Saratoga Passage.

Camano Island is connected to the mainland by a bridge at Stanwood. From the bridge, Hwy 532 continues three miles west to a directory for the island located at Terry's Corner. Here the road splits, with East Camano Drive to the left and North Camano Drive to the right. Terry's Corner is the reference point for directions to Camano Island sites listed in this book.

Terry's Corner landmark

Site 58 — ENGLISH BOOM HISTORICAL PRESERVE
Lat/Long: N 48° 15.740, W 122° 26.321

Directions: From Hwy 532 turn N onto Good Rd (about 2 miles E of Terry's Corner). Continue 1.9 miles as road turns W and becomes Utsalady Rd. Just past Camano Island Airfield, turn N (R) onto Moore Rd and drive 0.6 miles to road end. From west or south Camano Island, take Arrowhead Rd north to Utsalady Rd, turn R onto Utsalady and travel east, turning N (L) onto Moore Rd as above.

Parking: 6 cars, 2 ADA spaces. 10 more parking spaces on right 0.1 mile uphill from road-end parking area.

Adjoining public tideland: 300 feet, with trail easement to east across private land.

In clear weather this site has a spectacular view of Mt. Baker and the Cascades. The story of the logging days at English Boom is told at a historical kiosk. A 160-foot ADA-accessible boardwalk for wildlife viewing was completed in 2005 along with an open-sided shelter. Another trail leads through salt marsh to the end of the property and continues on an easement. The English Boom area, over 500 acres of salt marsh, mudflat and beach berm on the shore of Skagit Bay, offers habitat for waterfowl, shorebirds and raptors. Island County owns 7 acres near the west end of this area. Decaying pilings, reminders of a once extensive log storage system, provide perches for fish-hunting birds such as bald eagle, osprey, heron and kingfisher. You will likely see great blue herons from the nearby Davis Slough Heronry. Bird houses have been erected for purple martins, the largest North American swallow. At low tide, seals haul out on exposed sand banks.

Wheelchair-accessible boardwalk at English Boom Preserve

Ospreys carry their catch aerodynamically

Ospreys are the only North American raptors that feed exclusively on fish. And of the large raptors that nest in the Pacific Northwest, they are the only one that migrates south for the winter. Ospreys return in mid-April to build large stick platform nests in tree tops or on high platforms. Ospreys also nest on channel markers in harbors and a wide array of artificial sites, selecting sites where fishing is good.

Ospreys can only access the top two or three feet of water so they look for surface-schooling fish or shallow water. When an osprey spies its prey, it stretches both legs in front and dives toward the water. Grasping a fish with its sharp talons, the osprey flies on without landing. It then maneuvers the fish head-first into an aerodynamic flight position.

Great blue herons spear their food

With its long neck and legs, the great blue heron is a familiar sight standing sentinel on docks, hunkered on the mudflats or wading in shallow water.

When feeding, the great blue heron stands motionless in knee-deep water watching for fish, its long neck recoiled. Then in a surge of power the bird jabs its sharp bill into the water to spear a fish. If successful, the heron shuffles the fish into its beak and swallows it whole. Taking a few more steps, the great blue heron pauses again and assumes a frozen stance, eyes focused into the water. This adaptive species also stalks pastures and roadsides, hunting small mammals, reptiles, amphibians and insects.

Some Native American traditions hold that herons contain the souls of wise men who have returned to earth on mysterious pilgrimages. If true, these wise souls made a good choice: a magnificent bird with a quiet, reflective spirit capable of waiting, watching and seeing below the surface.

Site 59 | UTSALADY BEACH
Lat/Long: N 48° 15.213, W 122° 29.893

Directions: From Terry's Corner, follow North Camano Dr 2.9 miles. Turn N onto Utsalady Point Rd. Keep to R and proceed downhill 0.25 mile to parking area and boat launch. This access has close neighbors; please respect private property and do not park along road.
Parking: 10
Adjoining public tideland: 380 feet.

Utsalady Beach

This access has a single-lane concrete boat ramp. Beyond the parking area is a grassy area with several picnic tables. Two kayak camping sites at the east end have fire pits and stairs to the beach, with views across a scenic bay to Mt. Baker. Today Utsalady Bay is home to beachside houses and moored pleasure boats, but in the late 1800s it was a working port, home to a large sawmill. From here sailing ships carried lumber to world markets. Utsalady also served as a landing for the ferry between Camano and Whidbey Island (box, p.30).

Beach hoppers aren't fleas and don't bite

If you move aside a pile of washed up seaweed, chances are you'll see a flurry of wild random hopping by hordes of minute creatures. These are beach hoppers, tiny crustaceans that stay just above the water level as it moves up and down with the tides. Beach hoppers are sometimes called "sand fleas" but they're not fleas or even insects; they are crustaceans, related to shrimp. Nor do they bite. If you try to hold them in your hand, you may feel a sharp prickle. That's not their teeth but instead their feet, pointed to help them cling to the decomposing seaweed in which they feed and seek refuge.

© Jan Holmes

Site 60 UTSALADY VISTA PARK
Lat/Long: N 48° 15.343, W 122° 30.266

Directions: Follow directions for Site 59. From North Camano Dr turn N onto Utsalady Point Rd, then fork L on Shore Dr. The park is a couple hundred feet on the L.

Parking: 3 🏠 ⛩ 🧺

This grassy pocket park atop the bluff at Utsalady Point has picnic tables, a viewpoint, and a carved bas-relief historical marker depicting the sawmill era. There is no access to the beach.

Utsalady Bay and the sawmill era

Settlers in the 1850s relied heavily on canoes and other small craft, so they were quick to discover the merits of Utsalady Bay on the north end of Camano Island. It offered shelter from storms that typically blew from the southeast. Entrepreneurs soon recognized Utsalady Bay was an ideal site for a sawmill to handle timber as settlers cleared logjams on the Skagit River and harvested trees in northern Puget Sound. Thomas Cranney and Laurence Grennan built their sawmill here in 1858 and it remained open until 1890, shipping high-quality timber from the frontier to ports as distant as Europe and Asia. The mill became the hub of a community on north Camano Island that provided supplies and services to settlers from throughout the region.

Site 61 — MAPLE GROVE PARK
Lat/Long: N 48° 15.162, W 122° 31.062

Directions: From Terry's Corner, follow North Camano Dr 3.1 miles and take a lazy R turn onto Maple Grove Rd. The County Park with boat launch is 0.5 mile farther down the road. This access has close neighbors; please respect private property and park only in designated area.

Parking: 10-12

Adjoining public tideland: 250 feet at and west of road end.

Maple Grove Park

© Craig Johnson

The rocky shores of Maple Grove offer access to the Skagit estuary and a view of Mt. Baker. Cormorants can often be seen on the pilings drying their wings after a dive for fish. Polnell Point, on Whidbey Island east of Oak Harbor, is 3½ miles distant to the northwest.

Double-crested cormorant

Camano Island–A Community Wildlife Habitat

Camano Island enjoys a rare distinction–the entire island was the 10th community in the nation certified by the National Wildlife Federation (NWF) as a Community Wildlife Habitat. Camano was nationally certified in 2005 with 500 yards–many more have since been added. As more neighbors certify their yards, island residents create safe wildlife corridors as well as clean water resources.

A wildlife habitat provides four essential elements for wildlife to live in harmony with humans–food, water, shelter and places to raise a family. These may be present naturally or provided by the homeowner. Caretakers of certified properties also practice sustainable gardening techniques to improve the health of the soil, air, water and habitat for all.

Single and multi-family residences, businesses, schools, community areas, shorelines and demonstration gardens are individually certified to create a community that makes a place for wildlife. Additionally, islanders have become visible members of a network of thousands of people in the nation who share their living space with wildlife in yards and communities. Backyard habitats are a work in progress, ranging in size from a small deck to acres of land.

Applications and help are available from Friends of Camano Island Parks (FOCIP) habitat stewards, FOCIP Habitat Project, PO Box 1385, Stanwood, WA 98292, email camanobwh@yahoo.com, or from the NWF at www.nwf.org/backyardwildlifehabitat.

Backyard Wildlife Habitat certification is through the NWF. A small fee is charged for processing. Members receive a certificate and the NWF newsletter, Habitats, and a one-year subscription to National Wildlife Magazine.

Site 62	LIVINGSTON BAY (Fox Trot Way)
	Lat/Long: 48° 14.198, 122° 26.023

Directions: From Terry's Corner, travel 1 mile E on Hwy 532. Turn S onto Fox Trot Way and proceed straight 0.2 mile to the road end access.

Parking: 10-15

Adjoining public tideland: 90 feet (road width).

Livingston Bay, a mudflat at lower tides, can only be used by shallow draft boats, canoes or kayaks during the high tides. If you are caught in the bay in anything less than a high tide, you will certainly be like a fish out of water. A broad expanse of driftwood separates road end and tideland. The tussocks of marsh grass are the exotic weed spartina (box, p.28), which state and local agencies are fighting. Tide pools formed by spartina offer protection to juvenile fish, but the invasive grass robs tidelands of the ability to support shellfish and migratory bird populations. It also traps sediments over time, raising the level of the tidelands above sea level.

Clumps of invasive spartina grass grab a roothold in Livingston Bay

Kristoferson Creek–Camano Island's salmon stream

Tucked inside a sheltered right-angle bend on Camano Island's inside east shore is Triangle Cove, a large (200-acre) pocket estuary at the mouth of Kristoferson Creek. The creek drains the island's second largest watershed and is Camano's only salmon-bearing stream, supporting a small run of spawning chums in the late fall. Triangle Cove is important not just for fry from Kristoferson Creek, but also for the fry recently hatched in the Stillaguamish River on the mainland to the east. Juvenile coho and chinook have been observed rearing in the creek.

In 2005, Conservation Futures funding was dedicated to acquiring 2½ acres and nearly 255 feet along the lower reach of Kristoferson Creek above Russell Road. This will provide a publiclyowned location where school children and the general public can access the creek for education and wildlife viewing purposes.

Further upstream in the Kristoferson/Triangle watershed is an extensive beaver marsh. Much of the beaver marsh is privately owned, but public access is available at two points along Can Ku Road, across from the animal shelter. One-half block to the west of East Camano Drive, a short trail leads to a viewing platform which looks out over the lower part of the marsh. At the intersection of Can Ku Road and East Camano Drive, a trail leads to the "Beaver Deceiver," a water leveling device installed at the outlet of the beaver marsh by Island County to manage the water level to protect downstream properties while allowing the beaver to maintain their habitat. The beaver marsh habitat is important for flood control and water quality, as well as providing rearing habitat for juvenile coho.

Site 63 IVERSON SPIT PRESERVE
Lat/Long: N 48° 12.646, W 122° 26.544

Directions: (a) From Terry's Corner travel S on East Camano Dr for 2.7 miles to Russell Rd. Turn L, go 1 mile E on Russell, turn R onto Sunrise Blvd for 0.2 mile, then L onto Iverson Beach Rd for 0.3 mile. At stop sign turn L on Iverson Rd past a row of houses 0.25 mile to road end. (b) From Terry's Corner traffic light, turn S onto Sunrise Blvd for 2.5 miles, turn L onto Iverson Beach Rd and continue as above.

Parking: 5 🚻 🚶 🚣 🐦 🥾

Adjoining public tideland: None to south, 2,400 feet north to end of spit.

This mixture of marsh and farm fields at the southwest corner of Livingston Bay, historically a tidal salt marsh, was diked for farming in the 1940s. The 120-acre property was acquired by Island County in 1999 with Conservation Futures funding. A 1-mile loop trail takes the walker through wetland, thickets, lowland forest and field edges. Birds of water, shore and brush abound. A boardwalk with viewing platforms and boxed steps over the dike have been added to reduce erosion. The beach beyond a wide expanse of drift logs offers views of both Mt. Baker and Mt. Rainier. (Trail map p. 150)

Iverson Spit Preserve

Site 64 | CAVALERO PARK & BOAT RAMP
Lat/Long: N 48° 10.452, W 122° 28.622

Directions: From Terry's Corner, follow East Camano Dr 5.5 miles. Turn E onto Cavalero Rd and in 0.25 mile follow the signs L onto a narrow, steep, winding, single-lane road that drops down to the park.

Parking: 15-20

Adjoining public tideland: 250 feet at park.

This rocky shore gives way to a shallow sandy tideland at the lower tides, making it a popular swimming area. Cavalero Park is the only public launch on Camano Island that gives access to Port Susan and the Stillaguamish estuary. The boat ramp, usable only at high tide, is not appropriate for launching large boats due to the steep, single lane access road. It offers a scenic panorama from Mount Baker to Three Fingers mountain. Look for great blue herons roosting in trees along the bluff to the north or feeding in the bay at low tide.

When travel was an adventure

Early islanders traveled in style. The steamers Camano and Whidby carried passengers and freight daily among local communities from about 1906 – 1912. Both were built in Coupeville by Captain H.B. Lovejoy. This schedule appeared in The Camano Enterprise in 1907. The two vessels were lost in separate accidents after just a few years, but others picked up the slack. This was the era of the Mosquito Fleet of Puget Sound lore – the heyday of stern-wheelers, side-wheelers and propeller-driven craft. Early roads were primitive. Camano Island got its bridge to the mainland in 1909, but Whidbey went without till 1935. Most Camano passengers used the Camano "City" dock near Chapman Creek, by the current Camano Island Inn. A few remnants are still visible. Before a Mabana dock was built, Mabana passengers often rowed out to be picked up. The Whidbey stop called Saratoga was about four miles north of Langley.

Island Transportation Co.

Str. ,'Whidby" Time Card:

LEAVING

NORTH BOUND	SOUTH BOUND
Seattle..........4 P. M.	LaConner (Subject to
(Except Sat. and Sun.'	tide)
Sun. 3 p. m. touching	Utsaladdy...6;30 A. M.
Everett.)	Oak Harbor 7:15 "
Clinton......6:15 P. M.	San de Fuca 7:45 "
Langley.....6:45 "	Coupeville 8:30 "
Saratoga.....7:05 "	Camano..... 9:15 "
Camano......7:45 "	Saratoga....9:45 "
Coupeville...8:30 "	Langley....10:10 "
Oak Harbor...9:15 "	Clinton....10:35 "
	Arriv'g Seattle 1 P. M.

Str. "Camano" Time Card

(Daily except Sunday.)

LEAVING SOUTH BOUND

Coupeville........... ....7:00 A. M.
Oak Harbor.................. ....7:30 "
Camano .... 8:15 "
Langley .... 9:15 "
Clinton .... 9:45 "
Arriving at Everett...... .... 10:15 "

Leaving Everett for Coupeville, 3 P. M.

Brown's Point, San de Fuca and Saratoga, subject to call.

The steamer, Camano

Courtesy of the Puget Sound Maritime Historical Society.

Cama Beach and the heyday of Puget Sound fishing resorts

For centuries Salish Indians had a summer encampment at a particularly attractive point of land on Camano Island, today known as Cama Beach. Later it became a center of logging activity and in the 1930s was purchased to become Cama Beach Resort, one of the premiere Puget Sound family fishing resorts of the 1930s, '40s and '50s. Families rented summer cabins by the week and fished the nearby waters of Saratoga Passage from a fleet of small kicker boats maintained by the resort. Cama Beach closed its doors in 1989 but many of the cabins and buildings still remain. The park is currently under development by the state in cooperation with several Native American tribes and the Center for Wooden Boats.

Site 65 | CAMA BEACH STATE PARK
Lat/Long: 48° 08.717, 122° 30.554

Directions: From Terry's Corner, go S on East Camano Dr about 6 miles. When East Camano Dr heads L, keep R on main road which is now Elger Bay Rd. At Elger Bay Grocery and gas station, turn W onto Mountain View Rd (becomes West Camano Dr). Go 2.5 miles, up a steep hill, then follow West Camano Dr to the R and look for park entrance on L.

Cama Beach has over one mile of beach, 433 mostly-forested acres and a 5-acre lake with wetland. It is the site of a 2,000-year-old Native American summer encampment, a logging camp from the 1880s until 1906, and an auto court fishing resort from 1934 until 1989. Through purchase and donation, State Parks acquired the majority of the property in 1997. The park currently is under construction and plans to open in 2008. Contact the state park at 360-387-7542 or e-mail cama.beach@parks.wa.gov for more information.

Camano Island's Spanish name

Camano Island is named for Lt. Don Jacinto Caamano of the Spanish Navy who, during the 1700s, had explored as far north as Alaska from the Spanish naval base in San Blas, Mexico. However, Caamano never entered Puget Sound. The name was given in 1847 by a British surveyor as part of an effort to restore Spanish names in the area. The local Salish called it Kol-lut-chen, "land jutting out into a bay."

Getting to the Water's Edge 91

Site 66 | CAMANO ISLAND STATE PARK
Lat/Long: N 48° 07.275, W 122° 29.447

Directions: From Terry's Corner, go S on East Camano Dr about 6 miles. When East Camano Dr heads L, keep R on main road which is now Elger Bay Rd. At Elger Bay Grocery and gas station, turn W onto Mountain View Rd. Go 2 miles, up a steep hill, then turn L onto Lowell Point Rd and follow to park entrance.

The park provides many amenities. For information contact the state park (360-387-3031) or go to www.parks.wa.gov.

In 1949, 900 volunteers started the park in one day. Ever since it was established, Camano Island State Park has been Camano Island's most popular destination. Its 134 acres include a 3-lane boat ramp, 88 wooded campsites, rental cabins, two picnic shelters, and more than a mile of shoreline on Saratoga Passage offering beach walking, bird watching, swimming, year-round fishing, and an underwater park for scuba divers. Over 5 miles of trails and a self-guided nature trail appeal to hikers. An amphitheater offers interpretive programs throughout the summer. ADA-accessible restrooms are at the Group Camp and North Beach parking areas. The park is also the location of the first Washington Water Trails campsite, located at Lowell Point. (Trail map p. 155)

Camano Island State Park

Pocket estuaries–Island County's salmon nurseries

Even though Whidbey and Camano islands support no large river systems like the nearby Skagit, Stillaguamish or Snohomish, their relatively natural shorelines fill an important niche for juvenile salmon originating from those rivers. The islands' shorelines are dotted with many small coastal lagoons, called pocket estuaries. Typically, these are partially enclosed, often marshy areas where streams or fresh water outflows dilute the sea's normal salinity. Among the better known pocket estuaries on Whidbey Island are Ala Spit marsh, Harrington Lagoon and Hancock Lake. Pocket estuaries on Camano include Triangle Cove and Elger Bay. They are naturally rich, dynamic environments with a diversity of plants, insects, birds and other wildlife, and provide a transition zone in which juvenile salmon can rest, feed and adjust to changes in salinity. Increased awareness of their importance in recent years is leading to greatly increased

© Bill Blandin

Volunteers seining in Elger Bay

study. Seining surveys are underway in many Island County estuaries by such organizations as the Skagit River System Cooperative, WSU Beach Watchers, the National Oceanographic and Atmospheric Administration, Tulalip and Stillaguamish tribes, and by Washington Trout. They are studying not only which fish use these pocket estuaries, but how, and when, and how many.

Site 67 — TILLICUM BEACH
Lat/Long: 48° 06.203, 122° 23.990

Directions: From Terry's Corner, follow East Camano Dr south for 11.7 miles. Turn E onto Karen Way and continue 0.4 mile to bottom of hill. Turn L on Tillicum Beach Dr to access on water side with small parking area opposite.

Parking: 4 🏕 🛶

Adjoining public tideland: 80 feet of community beach dedicated to the public.

This pleasant, quiet pocket park in the middle of a small beach-front community provides a panoramic view of the Cascade Mountain Range. Please drive slowly and respect private property. Note that launching/landing a hand-carry boat may be difficult at high tide because of large quantities of driftwood that slosh against the shore.

Beach plants are well worth a look

When you get to the beach, don't forget to look at the backshore plants. This is the vegetation that grows high on the beach near the line marked by driftwood stranded during very high tides. Many of these plants serve an important role on the beach because their root systems help stabilize the sand.

Dunegrass

The native dunegrass (Elymus mollis), with blades more than three feet high and one-half inch wide, is blue-gray with a rather powdery texture. Dunegrass was used by indigenous peoples for weaving pack straps and baskets.

Both American and European sea rocket (Cakile edentula and C. maritima) are mustard family annuals inhabiting Island County beaches. Sea rocket is a pioneer species, among the first to move into areas of barren sandy dunes and has unique seed pods that pop apart into two sections when mature. One section remains attached to the parent plant to be buried by blowing sand and then to bring new growth in the same place the following season. The other section floats away with the tides to colonize new territory.

Look, too, for the yellow sunflower-like blooms that characterize the aptly-named gumweed (Grindelia integrifolia). The green bracts surrounding its flowers are covered with a white, very sticky latex or "gum."

On protected tideflats, beaches and salt marshes you may find the distinctive thick succulent stems of pickleweed (Salicornia sp.). One of its common names, glasswort, comes from a historical use of this plant; its salty stems were reduced to ashes to provide carbonate of soda, an ingredient in glassmaking.

Gumweed flower

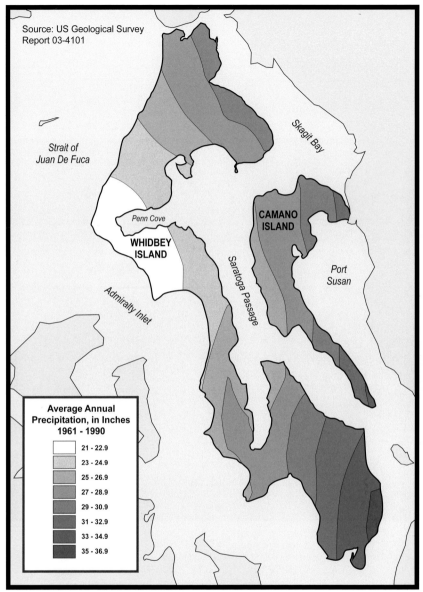

Source: US Geological Survey
Report 03-4101

Strait of
Juan De Fuca

Skagit Bay

Penn Cove

CAMANO
ISLAND

WHIDBEY
ISLAND

Saratoga Passage

Port
Susan

Admiralty Inlet

**Average Annual
Precipitation, in Inches
1961 - 1990**

21 - 22.9
23 - 24.9
25 - 26.9
27 - 28.9
29 - 30.9
31 - 32.9
33 - 34.9
35 - 36.9

*We are dry in the middle and wet on the ends. Rainfall varies annually from 21 to 37
inches on different parts of Whidbey and Camano islands, and microclimates abound.
This US Geological Survey rainfall map reveals big differences over a small area. The
Olympic Mountains shield the central part of both islands from west-approaching
storms, creating a dry "rain shadow." Central Whidbey's fertile agricultural prairies
are in the driest zone of all, once devoted to large dairy and wheat production, but
now trending toward smaller-scale specialty and organic farms. Farmers capitalize on
the drier and warmer winters to raise seed crops such as spinach, cabbage and beets.
Native vegetation reflects the moisture and soil conditions.*

CHAPTER FOUR

Guide to Intertidal Life

Written and photographed by Mary Jo Adams and Jan Holmes

Editor's note: For more about of intertidal species, visit www.beachwatchers.wsu. edu/island/ and click on Intertidal Organisms EZ-ID Guides.

INVERTEBRATES

Anemones

Early scientists thought anemones were half plant and half animal and it's easy to see why. When the tide covers them and they open, they look much like flowers. They are animals, however, and are in fact carnivores. Anemones have stinging cells in their tentacles, which they use to capture and subdue their prey. The most common species on Island County beaches is the **aggregating anemone** (*Anthopleura elegantissima*). It can grow as a solitary individual or in massive clumps of clones. If in a clump, all others in the clump will be genetically identical. This anemone's green or olive color comes from tiny algae and dinoflagellates that live in its soft tissues.

Aggregating anemone

Worms, worms, worms

Our intertidal area is littered with hundreds of worm-like creatures that take advantage of both soft sediment and rocky habitats. The most common species fall into three major groups: marine segmented worms (polychaetes), ribbon worms (nemerteans) and marine flatworms (polyclad turbellarians). **Polychaete** bodies are divided into multiple segments like earthworms. On most polychaetes, each segment is equipped with bristles embedded in flap-like outgrowths. A specie's segment structures reflect the lifestyle of the worm. It can be specialized for swimming, burrowing, tube building and other activities. Polychaete head appendages reflect the worm's diet and food gathering

Polychaete

habits. They range from elaborate "feather duster" plumes for catching plankton, to protruding jaws and teeth for tearing apart plant and animal material. Many polychaetes are also equipped with elaborate sensory apparatus.

Nemerteans or ribbon worms look like pieces of spaghetti or linguini. They have soft, fragile, ciliated bodies that can stretch for yards in some species. The distinctive feature of the group is the remarkable prey-capturing organ, the proboscis. When not in use it is tucked inside the animal like an inverted finger on a rubber glove. When stimulated by prey, the worm "fires" its proboscis using hydrostatic pressure. The proboscis shoots out, stabbing the victim with an attached poison stylet or encircling it with sticky "prey quieting" secretions. The prey is then engulfed in snake-like fashion. Many nemerteans prefer to eat polychaetes and can ingest animals several times their size.

Ribbon worm

Polyclad flatworms often cling to the undersides of rocks or other hard substrates. Their soft, flat, ciliated bodies look like tiny pieces of creeping, flattened, chewing gum. Their mouth is located in the center of the lower surface and most have conspicuous eyespots on the upper surface. Many flatworm species are known carnivores, feeding on various mollusks, crustaceans and other marine invertebrates. They evert their pharynx around the prey, then retract it inside to begin digestion. They do not have a complete digestive tract, so undigested material must be passed out through the mouth.

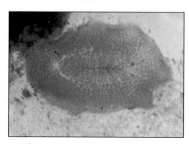

Flatworm

Snails

Among the more common snails on our beaches are the periwinkles, dogwinkles and moon snails. All have a raspy tongue-like organ called a radula with which they scrape and drill to procure their food. **Periwinkles** are small, less than an inch long and live on rocks high up in the intertidal. They crawl along, scraping algae off rocks with their radula. The somewhat larger **dog-**

Moon snail

winkles, on the other hand, are predators, feeding on mussels and barnacles. You might see clumps of what look like oats on intertidal boulders at certain times of the year. Those are the egg cases of dogwinkle snails. Fist-sized **moon snails** live on sandy beaches and spend most of their time plowing along just under the surface of the sand, seeking clams. When they find one they drill through its shell, leaving a circular hole with a countersunk appearance. After intertidal snails die their shells are often recycled as homes for hermit crabs.

Limpets

Limpets look like small, conical hats. As mollusks they are closely related to snails and chitons and, like them, use a combination of tongue and teeth called a radula. The **plate limpet** (*Tectura scutum*) has a very long radula that measures almost twice the length of its shell. Of course, most of the radula is kept tucked away and the creature uses only a small part of it when feeding.

Limpets are herbivores and make their living scraping thin films of diatoms and algae off intertidal rocks and other surfaces. Limpets are active only when covered by the tide, creeping along the surface of the rock with some species returning to a "home spot" before the water recedes. They may fall prey to crabs, sea stars and birds such as the oystercatcher.

Plate limpet

Chitons

Chitons (pronounced "kitons," rhyming with "titans") are related to limpets.

Lined chiton

Instead of one shell, however, they have eight overlapping plates held together by a girdle of tough tissue. This allows them to bend, flex and conform better to the shape of the rock they are on. Chitons use their radula to scrape algae and other small organisms off rocks. Island County is home to several species including the **gumboot chiton** (*Cryptochiton stelleri*), largest species in the world, growing to 13 inches and resembling a large meatloaf. Sometimes after a storm (especially on west Whidbey Island) gumboot chitons dislodged by the heavy seas can be found tossed up on the beach where they look like half a cantaloupe. Other chiton species found in this area are the colorful **lined chiton** (*Tonicella sp.*), the **black Katy chiton** (*Katharina tunicata*) and the **mossy chiton** (*Mopalia sp.*). If you find one please leave it attached to the rock. They cannot reattach very well and probably will not survive if pulled up.

Clams and mussels

Clams and mussels are mollusks belonging to the bivalve group, their shells being made of two halves joined by a hinge. One or two large muscles keep the shells pulled shut. Both clams and mussels are filter feeders, collecting plankton and other small particles from the water. The most obvious difference between them is that clams generally bury themselves in sand, mud or other substrate, while mussels are right out on the surface, adhering

Littleneck clam

to rocks, pilings or each other. Look closely at a mussel and you'll see hair-like strands holding it in place. Called byssal threads, these are secreted as liquid that solidifies into a filament when it comes in contact with salt water. Clams

Mussels

have a foot adapted for burrowing. As the clam extends its foot into the sand, the tip of the foot expands and serves as an anchor while the rest of the clam pulls itself down. If you dig clams, please fill the holes when you are finished. Otherwise, piles of sand left on the beach will smother other organisms that live beneath the surface.

Barnacles

Barnacles are crustaceans, relatives of shrimp, crabs and beach hoppers. Adult barnacles are permanently attached to some type of substrate, which varies with the species. Some, like the common acorn barnacle, can be found in the intertidal and resemble little stone rosettes attached to rocks. Others reside on the backs of whales and in odd places such as the species which lives on turtle tongues!

Stalked barnacles such as the "goose" barnacle live in body chambers attached to a flexible stalk or peduncle, anchored to a hard substrate. Prior to the 1800s some people thought goose barnacles developed into feathered geese!

Thatched barnacle

Unstalked barnacles such as the acorn barnacle have a flat base plate and hard calcareous overlapping side plates. The base plate is attached to the substrate with "barnacle cement," which is stronger than epoxy cement and capable of supporting 7,000 pounds with just one tiny dab. Barnacles knocked off their rock substrates will sometimes leave

Acorn barnacle

behind the white base plate giving the rock a "snowflaked" appearance.

Our common **acorn barnacle** (*Balanus glandula*) lives its adult life standing on its head inside its shell. When the barnacle is submerged in seawater, inner plates of the shell open up to expose the cirrus, a fan-like feeding appendage (actually modified legs), which the barnacle uses to comb the water for plankton. Like other crustaceans, the barnacle must periodically molt to increase in size (see B6). When this happens, the acorn barnacle also enlarges its shell home by dissolving part of the inside of the shell and adding on the outside.

Barnacles are hermaphrodites. Both male and female reproductive organs are present in each individual, but self-fertilization is not common. Barnacles begin life as bristly, one-eyed swimming larvae. When ready for attachment, they metamorphose into a second larval stage to find a suitable attachment spot. Once cemented in place they live as sedentary plankton feeders. Barnacles are harvested commercially for fertilizer and food in some areas. Goose barnacles are popular in Europe as a soup stock base. Barnacles on boat hulls are also a serious nuisance organism in maritime communities.

Pelagic gooseneck barnacle

Shore crabs

Now here's a feisty little guy – the shore crab (genus *Hemigrapsus*). Be ready to get your finger pinched if you pick one up.

Green shore crab

They have a rectangular-shaped carapace up to two inches wide, with three "teeth" along the edge behind each eye. Shore crabs are built low-to-the-ground so they can get under rocks for cover.

Hemigrapsus nudis, the **purple shore crab**, usually has purple spots on its claws. Though generally the carapace is purple, you might find one that is olive green or reddish brown, without the purple spots on the claws. Check the walking legs for hair. This species will be hairless. *H. nudis* tends to be found under boulders and in mussel beds on beaches with a fair amount of wave energy.

Hemigrapsus oregonensis, the **Oregon or green shore crab**, looks similar to *H. nudis* except it has no spots on its claws. Though usually green, carapace color is variable and in juveniles may be white. Look closely for the tiny, bristly hairs on the walking legs that distinguish this species from the purple shore crab. *H. oregonensis* can be found in areas with cobbles and under debris on mudflats. It tends to inhabit somewhat protected waters. *H. nudis* and *H. oregonensis* are sometimes both found on the same beach.

Do not confuse the green shore crab with the invasive **European green crab** (*Cancer maenas*). The European green crab belongs to a completely different genus and has a fan-shaped rather than rectangular carapace.

Sea stars

Several sea star species live in our waters. They may have five, six, or up to 24 rays and range from tiny to three feet across. Sea stars move on tube feet controlled by a water vascular system. Look for a spot near the center on their dorsal (top) surface. That is the madreporite, the plate through which seawater enters the vascular system. One of the most commonly found species on beaches where the waters are calm is the **mottled sea star** (*Evasterias troschelii*). It has five slender rays, may reach a foot accross, and comes in various colors. On high-energy beaches such as those on west Whidbey Island, watch for the **purple sea star** (*Pi-*

Purple sea star

saster ochraceus), also called ochre sea star; it can be purple or orange. It may also be a foot across but is much thicker bodied and, in spite of its name, is not always purple. If you find a sea star please leave it where it is. Pulling it up may damage its tube feet.

Sea urchins

Sea urchins, which look much like pincushions, are closely related to sea stars and sand dollars. They are herbivores and feed on seaweed. The shell is called a "test" and they have a unique mouthpart called an "Aristotle's lantern." Sea urchin spines are attached to the test via ball-and-socket joints that allow them to be used for mobility. The spines are also useful for burrowing and protection. Red, green and purple sea urchins can be found in local waters. All belong to the genus *Strongylo-centrotus*, which in Greek means "ball of spines," so they are well named. Some sea urchins live 200 years or longer.

Green sea urchin

Sand dollars

Sand dollars are related to sea stars, sea urchins and sea cucumbers in the phylum Echinodermata. All of these "spiny skinned" strictly marine animals have bodies organized around a water vascular system composed of chambers and canals leading to hundreds of tiny tube feet. Sand dollars have an internal shell composed of thousands of tightly fitting plate-like calcareous "little bones." The flat, ridged sand dollar body plows through sand with its tube feet, collecting small food particles that are channeled into food grooves leading to the mouth. Sand dollars will also orient themselves on edge, letting the plankton-rich water wash over their oral surfaces. If you pick up a living sand dollar, replace it gently on the sand mouth down.

Like urchins, sand dollars grind and chew their food with the remarkable

Sand dollar

Aristotle's lantern, an inverted cone of five hard pointed teeth. In areas where there is considerable wave action, sand dollars accumulate iron in little internal pockets that serve as weight belts to help stabilize them. In crowded conditions, sand dollars have been observed dislodging other invertebrates and driving them out of sand dollar territory.

Live sand dollars are a rich dark brown or purple with soft felt-like bodies. They are often buried just below the surface in the low intertidal and can easily be overlooked until the beachcomber feels "cookie crunching" underfoot. Dead specimens are hard and white and often found washed ashore.

SEAWEEDS

Seaweeds are large marine algae attached to the sea floor or other substrate by a holdfast. They are non-vascular plants without true roots, stems or leaves. Three common species on our shorelines are bull kelp, rockweed and sea lettuce.

Bull kelp

Just off shore is a forest of seaweed complete with underbrush and canopy layer. One of the "tall trees" of this forest is the brown seaweed *Nereocystis luetkeana*, or bull kelp. But unlike terrestrial trees, bull kelp attains its giant length in just one growing season. It is among the fastest growing photosynthesizing species on the planet, adding about five inches a day and reaching lengths of almost 40 feet (with record specimens up to 118 feet).

Like other seaweeds, bull kelp has no roots and receives no nutrients from the substrate on which it lives. The long blades at the end of its stipe (stem) soak up nutrients directly from seawater. A large gas-filled bulb at their base

Bull kelp

keeps the long fronds afloat. Bull kelp forests provide a safe haven for juvenile fish and a host of invertebrates living on the bottom and in the water column. The kelp is eaten by relatively few animals, (among them green sea urchins which relish it), but provides a rich source of nutrients at the end of its life when it breaks down into small detritus particles. Detritus, and the protein-rich microbial colony attached to it, is consumed by a wide variety of marine animals. Humans also consume bull kelp. The blades and stipes are loaded with protein and vitamins and are a favorite ingredient in Asian cooking. Gulls, ducks and other birds sometimes perch on floating kelp blades, and great blue herons use the kelp beds as a platform from which to fish.

Rockweed

Fucus gardneri, or rockweed, is widely present along the northern Pacific Ocean. In rocky areas it forms a dense, low-growing canopy that protects numerous invertebrates and other seaweeds from drying out during low tide.

When uncovered by the tide it is a supple yellow-brown. With increased exposure time it will darken and become brittle, but rockweed has a high tolerance for exposure extremes. With the exception of small periwinkle snails, few invertebrates eat rockweed because of the polyphenols in its tissues, which bind to and inactivate digestive enzymes of the grazer. On the ends of its branches, mature rockweed has swollen air-filled sacs containing reproduc-

tive cells. Popping these little "balloons" on rockweed washed up on the beach is a favorite children's pastime.

Rockweed is used for poultry meal, fertilizer and garden mulch. Rockweed has been consumed by Native Americans for hundreds of years. A favorite way to consume it is when the swollen tips are hard and dry like marine popcorn!

Rockweed

Sea lettuce

This translucent, bright green, leafy seaweed is commonly found during the spring and summer at the mid to low tide level. Sea lettuce and its many green-bladed relatives can tolerate marine water that has been diluted, so look for it near freshwater sources. It is a fast growing opportunistic species and in some cases can over-grow everything around it. When these "blooms" occur, seaweeds underneath are deprived of light and the toxic low-oxygen conditions produced when the sea lettuce breaks down can wipe out entire invertebrate and fish communities. Like many other seaweeds, sea lettuce contains compounds which discourage grazing on it. These are not harmful to humans, however, and sea lettuce is another favorite seaweed in Asian cooking. It is a good source of vitamin C and rich in protein, iron and iodine.

If you collect sea lettuce or other seaweeds be sure you are far from potential sources of pollution. Over-harvesting or careless cutting of seaweeds can seriously damage a shoreline ecosystem, and whole areas have been denuded of these important algae. Most state park beaches are closed to seaweed harvest, and elsewhere certain seasons and maximum daily limits apply. A license from Washington Department of Fish & Wildlife is required to collect seaweed. This is the same license used for shellfish harvesting. Bull kelp must be cut a minimum of 24 inches above the bulb, and short-stemmed kelps at least 12 inches above the anchor point. These rules protect the ability of the seaweeds to reproduce, ensuring their continued presence in the area.

© Sally Slotterback

CHAPTER FIVE

Exploring the Edge

Go kayaking for a quiet, close view of nature

Kayaking is a tranquil way to experience the beauty and diversity of the islands' special places. It brings us quietly close to nature and affords time to see, hear, and smell, and take pictures with minimal disturbance of the setting.

Prepare carefully for a safe trip

Please understand that the rapidly changeable weather, currents, tides and winds around Whidbey and Camano islands require great respect, careful preparation and wise judgment. As a kayaker you are responsible for your own safety. Never kayak alone. Always check tides and currents before setting out. Tides cause currents but currents do not necessarily follow tides. So kayakers should consult not only a tide table but also a current table. Wind is a particular concern, as the *waters can change from flat calm to three-foot breaking waves within 10 to 15 minutes.* When surf picks up, exiting the water can be especially dangerous as large drift logs slam against the shore.

Make sure you are trained in safety procedures and have practiced self-rescue and re-entry. Puget Sound's numbingly cold year-round water temperatures can quickly disable persons in the water, allowing little time for rescue. Wear a wet- or dry-suit in addition to layered and windproof clothing. Be aware that rain and wet clothing can drain heat from your body and cause hypothermia, even without immersion. Wear a life jacket: state law *requires* that life jackets be worn by youth under 12 years old and carried in watercraft by all others. But because of Puget Sound's cold water temperatures all kayakers should wear, rather than carry, them. Carry first aid supplies and fire-making equipment in watertight containers. Do **not** consume alcohol. Share your kayaking plan with a friend or neighbor and let them know when you have safely returned. Consult a safety manual for additional advice about adequate floatation compartments, bailing equipment, towline, repair kits, signaling devices, radios and other safety measures.

Give marine mammals and birds their space

Even a low-impact activity such as kayaking can interfere with marine mammals and birds. Take care not to disturb bird roosts and seal haulouts. The Marine Mammal Protection Act requires all craft to stand back at least 100 yards – the length of a football field. Seals need time out of water to keep warm. Frightening them into the water causes stress and can be harmful. The law requires maintaining at least 200 yards from designated bird sanctuaries such as Protection Island. Binoculars are the best way to get a closer look.

Here are descriptions of some kayak routes around Island County. Site numbers refer to site descriptions in Chapter 3.

WHIDBEY ISLAND

The direction and velocity of both wind and current matter a great deal when kayaking Whidbey Island's shoreline, as does knowledge of how tide height affects launching sites. It helps to have a car at both your starting and ending points so you won't have to struggle against strong winds or currents back to your starting point. You can perhaps start your day at a launch point best used only at high tide and end at one where the tide level is not a serious issue – or vice versa.

The suggestions we include here were compiled by two Beach Watchers who kayaked all of Whidbey Island's 150 miles of shoreline over a four-year period, except for the especially challenging and dangerous waters of Deception Pass. The pass and nearby waters should not be attempted by any but the most qualified and experienced kayakers, preferably with an experienced guide after careful preparation.

Ala Spit (Site 5)

Pack a picnic lunch and enjoy a full day. Paddle to and around Hope Island, a Washington State Park Natural Area Preserve. It is about ⅓ mile from Ala Spit to Hope Island. After crossing the channel, paddle the north side of the island and go ashore at the bay landing site to enjoy your picnic and explore designated trails. If you paddle the south shoreline of the island on your way back to the spit you will encounter thick kelp beds as you approach the west side. The current is swift on the west shoreline, so consider staying in the kelp beds to make headway and for safety. Think about launching from and returning to Ala Spit at a fairly high tide, as at low tide you will find yourself transporting your kayak a considerable distance to and from the parking lot. Also consider crossing the channel between Whidbey and Hope islands at slack tide, as the current in the center of the channel also runs swiftly. An alternative way to enjoy this area is to launch at the Deception Pass State Park dock in Cornet Bay (Site 3) on an incoming tide (flood tide), and end your day at Ala Spit, leaving a car in both places. First paddle east, then south around Hoypus Point, a shoreline where you'll probably see sandpipers and other shorebirds. From Hoypus you can paddle out and catch a flood current over to Skagit Island and then paddle down to and around Hope Island. Enjoy your picnic lunch on either Hope Island or Skagit Island. Birding is excellent around and on both islands. End your adventure by paddling across the channel from Hope Island to Ala Spit when the tide level is relatively high, landing on the sandy, south-facing side of the spit.

West Penn Cove (Sites 22, 23, 26)
This is truly a delightful place, offering beautiful views of historic Coupeville from the water. It is easy to launch at any of the three sites. Paddle around Coupeville Wharf and observe the numerous sand dollars west of the wharf, the many sea stars attracted to the mussels on the pilings, as well as moon and egg yolk jellyfish floating in the water. The mussel rafts one mile west are fascinating when mussels are being harvested, cleaned and packed, but please respect this private property. Harbor seals and their pups often lounge on these rafts. Just another half-mile further is the historic Captain Whidbey Inn, a possible lunch stop. You may glimpse innkeeper John Colby Stone's classic 52-foot ketch, *Cutty Sark*. Penn Cove is designated as an Important Bird Area by Audubon Washington. You'll see ducks, loons and grebes on the water, shorebirds and great blue herons along the beaches and rocky shores as well as in Grasser's Lagoon, and raptors sailing overhead. If you launch during race week in July, you'll be entertained by about 150 sailboats flying colorful spinnakers. Please be careful to stay clear of the race course.

Ebey's Landing (Site 28)
If possible, launch from this site on a calm day or before the surf comes up, unless you are agile enough to jump into your kayak between waves in water up to your knees. Also, the walk to the water's edge will be shorter and easier if you launch at high tide. Wind and current direction and velocity make a difference, too, if you are planning to make this kayaking adventure one that is between Ebey's Landing and Fort Ebey State Park (Site 21). This is a pleasant paddle with lovely views of Ebey's Bluff from the water and abundant shore birds, harlequin ducks, bald eagles and northern harriers. If you are new to the area, a nice interlude from paddling is to go ashore briefly at Perego Lagoon along the way to view both the lagoon and wildlife around it. The beach at Fort Ebey State Park is a reasonably easy place to either launch, or end, your excursion. Just be aware that the walk back to the parking lot is uphill and a little long. If it's easier to carry your kayak downhill than uphill, launch at Fort

Ebey State Park and haul out at Ebey's landing, if the wind and currents will allow you to do so.

Keystone Jetty (Site 30)
Launch at the boat ramp in the harbor. Note that when tides are extreme, the current can be strong at the end of the jetty. The waters along the east side of the jetty and extending to the wooden pier are a marine conservation area popular with divers. The marine life is extraordinary; divers report more than 50 fish species and 40 invertebrate species including the giant Pacific octopus. It is also fun to poke around the abandoned wooden pier where marine life is abundant on the pilings and birds congregate on top. Pigeon guillemots nest in crevices of the old pier in summer; all three species of cormorants perch on top. For a longer paddle, launch at Ebey's Landing (Site 28) and head south to the harbor. Be sure to watch for the ferry and be very careful of the tricky shoals just to the west of the harbor entrance. Another alternative, especially attractive if you have two cars, is to continue south to Ledgewood Beach (Site 33).

Ledgewood Beach (Site 33)
This launch site requires carrying the boat down a few narrow steps to the beach but it's an especially enjoyable place to kayak if you have time for only a short excursion. Paddle north around some big rocks for good looks at intertidal invertebrates and a nice variety of brown algae nearby. The lion's mane jellyfish may be seen in this area.

Bush Point Boat Launch (Site 38)
Launch from this site at a minus outgoing tide (-2 or below) on a day when there is virtually no wind and the water is clear. You'll want to paddle north close enough to the shore to keep just 3-6 feet (or less) of water under your kayak. Beginning about ¼ mile or so from your launch point and extending for at least another ¾ mile north are perhaps the most incredible displays of brown algae Whidbey's waters offer from above water. Easily identified algae species firmly attached to rocks and flourishing along this shoreline include *Alaria marginata, Costaria costata, Iridea cordata, Laminaria saccharina* and *Sargassum muticum.* Amongst the blades of brown algae you are likely to be further treated to views of jellyfish, sea cucumbers, crabs and countless other possible species, if just for a fleeting moment. No glass-bottomed buckets or scuba gear are needed here to view nature's underwater splendor! Rhinoceros auklets and pigeon guillemots may also be seen above water in this area. It is a good idea to both begin and end this kayaking excursion at Bush Point, as the currents are often wildly confused and difficult to deal with at Lagoon Point, about 3 miles north of Bush Point.

Holmes Harbor (Site 41)

Put in at Freeland County Park and paddle out around Baby Island at the mouth of Holmes Harbor. Know your tides, or you could become separated from the dock by a broad expanse of dangerous, unwalkable mudflats. Baby Island is a haulout place for harbor seals and their pups. Keep at least 100 yards away and avoid approaching them. But they are very curious and may choose to approach you, swimming under the boat and popping their heads out of water to look at you. The paddle from Freeland is quite long but you may get a push on the return by a breeze from the north. You can also reach Baby Island by launching at Hidden Beach (Site 34). Paddling to Baby Island requires crossing the mouth of Holmes Harbor, an open-water crossing of about 1½ miles.

Double Bluff

Launch at Sites 43, 44 or 46 and paddle around Double Bluff. Plan with the tides because the intertidal flats at Double Bluff extend way out from the beach. At a very low tide it is a l-o-n-g walk back to the parking lot! Great beds of bull kelp grow right off Double Bluff itself. The seabird life is rich; scoters, harlequin ducks and pigeon guillemots are just a few of the birds you'll see in the water. In summer pigeon guillemots nest in burrows in the bluffs toward Mutiny Bay. Bald eagles frequent the trees on the bluff.

Langley Boat Harbor (Site 50)

You can launch from and return to this site at either a low or high tide without much worry. And depending on the wind and current velocity and direction, you can have a nice paddle either north or south. If you go south, expect to see shorebirds, loons, Bonaparte's gulls, western grebes and bald eagles on and around Sandy Point. Along the way, a lovely shoreline with overhanging trees will delight you. In spring, if you paddle north a few miles and the tide is out, you may spot gray whale feeding pits in the exposed mud and sand along the shoreline below the bluffs and high banks. Or you might be lucky enough to actually see a few gray whales! Be careful just offshore from the town of Langley at low tide. If you get hung up on the soft muddy bottom, you will not be able to step out of your kayak and re-launch yourself in deeper water.

Dave Mackie Park (Site 52)

Time your launch from (and possible return to) this site close to a high tide, as once again it is a long walk between solid ground and the parking lot at low tide! After determining the direction and velocity of wind and current, decide whether you want to paddle north or south. For a short excursion, after which you can easily return to this launch site, paddle north through shallow waters to view what appears to be a nursery for sand dollars. There are thousands!

Also consider coming down to this beach at a very low tide *before* your paddling adventure to view (from the shore) fascinating sandbars about ¾ mile north of Dave Mackie Park that could easily be mistaken as runways for small aircraft under certain circumstances, and then plan your paddle when you can coast over these particular sandbars in just a few feet of water. For a longer paddle, plan on heading south to Possession Beach Park (Site 57) and have a car in place so you can return to your start point by land. This route will take you around an extensive berm just slightly north of Cultus Bay that is used as a resting place by hundreds of gulls. The water is very deep just off this berm and bull kelp is abundant. If you are clear about the timing of the high and low tides, slip into Cultus Bay. This bay empties almost completely at low tide – and quickly! Then continue south around Possession Point and end your trip at the dock in Possession Beach Park. You can bring your car right up to the boat launch in this park. Alternately, launch at Possession Beach Park and end at Dave Mackie Park if the predicted tides, winds and currents favor a long excursion in a south-to-north direction that day.

Fidalgo Island
Editor's note: Just north of Deception Pass in Skagit County is another great kayaking opportunity not to be overlooked.

Bowman Bay and Rosario Head (Map p. 138)
Bowman Bay and Rosario are part of Deception Pass State Park on Fidalgo Island. Bowman Bay is easily reached from Highway 20; about ½ mile north of Deception Pass turn west on Rosario Rd, then take the first L. This is a good place to launch at any tide and is superb for protected paddling. Rosario Park is further down Rosario Rd, but you will have a long carry to launch there. Bowman Bay is a much better launch site. In good conditions this is a relatively safe paddle if you are mindful not to venture south of Bowman Bay entrance, which will bring you too close to the entrance of Deception Pass.

Head west out of the bay and turn north to take in the view of Rosario Head, exploring the exposed rocks along the way. Paddling in this area is especially enjoyable at low tide, where you can meet the sea creatures other boaters miss out on. Unlike the glacial substrates that comprise most of Island County's bluffs and beaches, this area is exposed bedrock. The steep rocks and sheer cliffs reveal a rich diversity of intertidal life including Christmas anemones (*Urticina crassicornis*), chitons, predatory dogwinkle snails, the breadcrumb sponge, and handsome purple and orange sea stars, *Pisaster ochraceus*. A large bed of bull kelp rings Rosario Head and a variety of other seaweeds can be seen growing on the rocks. Explore the exposed rocks and along the sea wall and then turn in toward Rosario beach. If you're lucky, you may get a good look at the resident oystercatchers–large black shorebirds with bright red bills and feet–that nest on the small islands northwest of Rosario Head. Take care not to disturb them. Continuing north about ¼ mile you'll come to a small cave. Nose your kayak in and visit more critters, again best at low tide. Huge white plumose anemones, *Metridium senile,* adorn the walls.

CAMANO ISLAND

Around Camano Island the tide and winds, more than currents, determine where and when to kayak. It is particularly important to note comments about tide levels. We offer some suggestions for kayak excursions from public access points. In most cases the next nearest launch/landing site has been noted for those with a shuttle car.

In 2002, to complete a survey of shoreline hardening, Washington State University (WSU) Beach Watchers walked Camano Island's entire perimeter with a Global Positioning System. The data gathered have been compiled into a database with descriptions of the shoreline, and some photos. This can be quite helpful when planning a kayak trip. The database is available at www.island.wsu.edu/camano/harden.

English Boom Preserve (Site 58)
English Boom Preserve accommodates launching/landing a kayak only at higher tides as there is an extensive area of tide flats. At higher tides, however, it does offer the closest launch/landing for the mouth of the West Pass of the Stillaguamish River. (See also Site 59.)

Utsalady Beach (Site 59)
Utsalady boat ramp is usable at all tide levels. It is heavily used by power boaters and also commercial crab boats, so parking can be very tight. Paddling to the east and then north around the bluffs of Arrowhead Point brings the kayaker into Skagit Bay. Time the tides carefully and you can have a ride up to English Boom Preserve (about 4 miles) and on into the mouth of the Stillaguamish River, then back to Arrowhead Point. The further east you paddle from Arrowhead Point the more tide flats, so it is important to check your tides. At mid to low tides you may see seals hauled out on sand islands in the middle of Skagit Bay. Paddling to the west and south around Utsalady Point brings you to Maple Grove Park in about 3½ miles.

Maple Grove County Park (Site 61)
Maple Grove offers a paved boat ramp good for launching at low tide. Parking is ample. Paddling east and north reveals an intertidal area of clay-like soil with shallow pools. Inside the pools are hundreds of anemones. This is

the closest Camano Island comes to tide pools. Continuing east around rocky Utsalady Point past shoreside homes, you come to Utsalady Beach.

Livingston Bay (Site 62)
Fox Trot Way provides kayak launching only at higher tides because of extensive mudflats, and only after a carry over considerable driftwood. The main attraction of Livingston Bay is bird watching, as it provides habitat for many water birds. A determined paddler could launch/land here and paddle 2-3 miles to Iverson Spit, which also has extensive tideflats and a considerable carry over driftwood.

Iverson Spit (Site 63)
See Livingston Bay above. Paddling south from Iverson Spit you pass several communities of shoreside homes, then travel around the bluffs of Barnum Point. Exploring Triangle Cove is a possibility, as is taking out at Cavalero Park in about 3 miles.

Cavalero Park (Site 64)
Cavalero Park has a boat ramp, and though there are some tide flats, it is possible to launch a kayak at all tides. Paddling north and east along Driftwood Shores spit, the reason for the name is very evident. At the east end of the spit is the entrance to Triangle Cove. It is possible to enter Triangle Cove at all tides but the best paddling is from mid to high tides. This is a favorite area to observe various birds in season. Eagles and heron are commonly seen fishing the channels, and various ducks and seabirds feed on the tide flats. Washington Department of Fish & Wildlife has been working to eradicate the invasive spartina grass and is making considerable progress. An energetic paddler could continue on to Iverson Spit if the tides were favorable.

Paddling south brings you along bluffs where the houses sit high above, after which you pass the shoreline homes of the Country Club development.

Camano Island State Park [CISP] (Site 66)
The boat launch at CISP is a good place to launch a kayak at any tide level. Paddling to the north several miles you can view the future Cama Beach State Park, with its 1930s-era cabins, boathouse and store. Cama Beach is expected to open in 2008. This stretch of Saratoga Passage is subject to afternoon winds and experiences heavy pleasure boat traffic close to shore, so keep an eye out for waves from the boat wakes. This is an area of fairly steep gravel beaches so tide level is not a concern.

Paddling to the south, then east around Pt. Lowell, brings the kayaker to one of the few areas on Camano with kelp beds. Continue east along the shore to Elger Bay. In the spring, look for eagles and sometimes gray whales.

Elger Bay has tide flats, but at mid to high tide it is possible to explore up into the blind channels behind the Elger Bay spit.

Tillicum Beach (Site 67)

Tillicum Beach requires a carry over driftwood, which makes launches/landings questionable at high tide. If the tide is out a bit, there is a nice gravel beach. Tide flats are only a problem at the very lowest tides. From this residential area it is possible to paddle along the shore in either direction. Paddling to the north takes you along residential areas, some at water level and others up on the bluff. Cavalero Park is approximately 6 miles. Paddling south you pass houses right on the water, then on to an area that has little noticeable human intrusion until you round the south tip at Camano Head. Camano Head shows evidence of a large landslide resulting from a local tsunami many years ago. After rounding Camano Head, you are again paddling along residential areas.

KAYAK CAMPS

Eleven kayak camps are listed by the Washington Water Trails Association in Island County or nearby waters. These campsites are intended only for those arriving by water in a non-motorized boat. They are among more than 50 such camps located along the Cascadia Marine Trail, a salt water trail spanning more than 140 miles from the Canadian border to southernmost Puget Sound near Olympia. This inland sea trail is a National Recreation Trail, designated by the White House as one of only 16 National Millennium Trails. Campsites are suitable for day use or multi-day trips, and may be reached from many public and private launch sites or shoreline trailheads. More information is available online from the Washington Water Trails Association, www.wwta.org/. Kayak camps are located at:

+ Deception Pass State Park (Bowman Bay) (Map p. 138)
+ Hope Island Marine Park
+ Skagit Island State Park
+ Ala Spit, Site 5
+ Windjammer Park, Site 14
+ Joseph Whidbey State Park, Site 16
+ Fort Ebey State Park, Site 21
+ Captain Coupe Park, Site 26
+ Possession Point State Park, Site 57
+ Utsalady Beach, Site 59
+ Camano Island State Park, Site 66

View whales from shore in spring and fall

Spring and fall are the top whale-watching seasons in Island County, though sightings are possible year-round. Gray whales and orcas visit the Whidbey and Camano shorelines every year, and when present may be seen from almost any place that offers a good view of the water.

In the spring, a small group of *seasonally resident gray whales* visits our waters from March through early June, especially Saratoga Passage, where they feed in areas of sandy or muddy shallows. On Whidbey Island, best places to look for gray whales are in Penn Cove (Sites 19, 23-27), from Hidden Beach (Site 34) north of Greenbank, in the sandy shallows directly off the Langley waterfront and marina (Sites 49, 50), and at Possession Point on the southern tip of the island (Sites 56-57). On Camano Island, best viewing typically occurs along the west side, especially the more southern parts (Sites 65, 66).

In the fall, *resident orcas* are seen off west Whidbey Island and occasionally in Saratoga Passage, usually during October through January. *Transient orcas* occasionally travel through Saratoga Passage and Port Susan, and can show up any time of year. Best places to view orcas on Whidbey Island are West Beach Vista (Site 17), Libbey Beach (Site 20), Fort Ebey (Site 21), Ebey's Landing bluff (Site 28), Fort Casey (Site 29), Lagoon Point (Sites 35, 36), Bush Point (Sites 38, 39), Clinton pier or ferry dock (Site 54), Glendale (Site 55) and Possession Point (Sites 56-57). On Camano Island, the west side occasionally offers orca viewing opportunities (Sites 65, 66).

Please report whale sightings to a toll-free number, 1-866-ORCANET, or e-mail reports to info@orcanetwork.org. Orca Network provides data collected through their Whale Sighting Network to The Center for Whale Research, The Whale Museum and the National Oceanographic and Atmospheric Administration (NOAA) Fisheries. To be on the Whale Sightings e-mail list, sign up now at www.orcanetwork.org.

© David Ellifrit

Fish for dinner or just for peace

Many beaches on the western shore of Whidbey Island offer exceptional shore fishing. For more about this, see the box on page 58. The hours spent fishing are a priceless opportunity to do some clear thinking, learn about nature, make a new friend and teach a child good habits.

Courtesy and etiquette keep anglers welcome

Some of the most welcome anglers on the beach are those who keep the big picture in mind. They politely ask permission, offer a hand to others, give space to their neighbor and pick up debris. They know that a few minutes of courtesy make all the difference in keeping recreational opportunities open. They take only the fish they will consume, use proper catch-and-release methods, and pick up stray monofilament line and hooks, leaving the beach cleaner and safer for wildlife and humans who will follow. They promote ethical behavior and public awareness of conservation issues. They not only catch fish but make it their business to be advocates for the fish, and for healthy marine habitat.

Find when and where to fish for salmon, how to identify our five salmon species, current regulations and other resources at www.wdfw.gov/fish/salmon/index.htm

Some Island County fishing beaches

Site	Name	Site	Name
1	Deception Pass State Park (salt and fresh water)	35	Lagoon Point North
		36	Lagoon Point South
2	Cornet Bay County Dock	37	South Whidbey State Park
3	Cornet Bay Boat Launch Pier	38	Bush Point Boat Launch
5	Ala Spit	39	Bush Point - Sandpiper Road
11	Oak Harbor City Marina	43	Mutiny Bay Shores
12	Pioneer Way East	47	Lone Lake
13	Flintstone Park	48	Goss Lake
21	Fort Ebey State Park	50	Langley Fishing Pier
22	Grasser's Lagoon	53	Deer Lake
28	Ebey's Landing	54	Clinton Beach Pier
29	Fort Casey State Park	56	Possession Point State Park
31	Keystone Spit	57	Possession Beach Waterfront Park
32	Driftwood Beach Park	63	Iverson Spit Preserve
		66	Camano Island State Park

Go clamming for buried treasure

Clamming is like going after treasure—you might get lucky. It is good family fun and great eating. It is easy to get caught up in the hunt for these bivalves that lurk underfoot, just out of sight. But please know what you are doing so you won't unintentionally kill more clams and other marine life than the entire harvest you take home. And please respect private property by staying within public beach boundaries. This will help keep clamming open.

1. Rule one – stay alive. Make *certain* the beach where you plan to dig is not closed. Know the status of the beach for *both* biotoxins and pollution. **Biotoxin closures: 1-800-562-5632,** state marine biotoxin hotline, or www. doh.wa.gov/ehp/sf/recshell.htm. Paralytic shellfish poisoning (PSP) is a lethal toxin sometimes present in shellfish, not destroyed by cooking or freezing. Only professional testing can detect it. Educate yourself about its symptoms and always call the biotoxin hotline before digging. **Viruses, bacteria or chemicals: 360-679-7350,** Island County Health Department. Check their website, www.islandcounty.net/health/ for more information on shellfish safety and closures. Find shellfish in the subject index. **Seasonal closures, resource conservation, crab and shrimp harvest information: 1-866-880-5431,** state Department of Fish & Wildlife hotline, or www.wdfw.wa.gov/fish/shellfish/beachreg/.

2. Get a license and display it properly. To ensure clams for future generations the state must track the harvest. So the law requires a personal-use shellfish license before harvesting on public beaches. During harvest, display it on the *outside* of your clothing. Before you go, carefully consult *Sport Fishing Rules for Washington,* published by the Washington Department of Fish & Wildlife (WDFW), available at hardware stores and other shellfish license outlets. It provides details on seasons, limits, safety closures and other rules. Pick it up when you buy your license.

3. Refill all the holes you dig. This is the law, but do it because it is right. Nearby clams, oysters and other marine life may suffocate under piles of sand or rocks, deprived of the seawater they require. Please push any undersized clams into the refilled hole (see next paragraph). Many immature clams are lost to currents and gulls from unfilled holes. They are a hazard to small children, adults and mobility-impaired individuals who may walk or wade on the uneven beach.

4. Replace clams properly. As you refill the hole, do your best to replace any undersized or excess clams as you found them. Place the clam with its siphons (neck) up and its foot down, no deeper than the length of its neck. To tell

which way is up when the shell is closed, note the bulge just below the hinge. The growth rings radiate from this bulge. The clam's neck protrudes above the hinge. Always replace a clam vertically, with the bulges (cheeks) below the hinge.

Rules to remember for replacing clams:
1. Place vertically, with cheeks below the hinge.
2. Place no deeper than twice the length of its shell.

The neck must reach the surface to extract food and oxygen from the water. Most clams cannot right themselves nor dig upwards, so if you put them back wrong, they will die. For example, a two-inch clam buried eight inches deep, or with its neck pointing down or sideways, will not survive. Usually you'll find the Manila littleneck within the first 1 – 4 inches below the surface, the native littleneck about 4 – 8 inches down, and butter clams 8 – 14 inches deep. Replace each clam at its proper depth – no deeper than twice the length of its shell.

5. Know your clam types, limits and habits. Knowing about the clam you're after can save a lot of trouble and damage to the resource. Can you recognize the size and shape of the holes it leaves? How deep does it go? Which shovel or tool works best? Which direction will it dig, so you won't dig into it and break it in half? Can it re-plant itself if you don't keep it? If the harvest regulation limit is 10 pounds or 40 clams, can you visualize 10 pounds of this particular clam? Learn more from classes given by WSU Beach Watchers, www.beachwatchers.wsu.edu/island/.

6. Carry a bucket – for clams *and* safety. Walking on saturated lower beaches and tide flats can feel downright *weird*. But it can quickly turn *scary* and then *terrifyingly dangerous*. At times it is impossible to stand or walk on tidal mud without becoming sucked in. A bucket's wide base can be a safety tool to help you gain leverage to pull your foot out of the mud. If you try to turn around you'll get sucked deeper, so back up, retracing your steps.

7. Handle and store your catch safely. The county health department recommends:

- ✦ **Rinse** your catch in salt water, not fresh, and cool it quickly on ice or in a refrigerator.
- ✦ **Cook** thoroughly, as soon as possible.
- ✦ **Wash** all seaweed before eating.
- ✦ **Store** all fresh shellfish in an open container in the refrigerator under a damp towel to maintain humidity. Never store in water more than two hours. They will die and may spoil. Maximum storage times vary:
  - ▶ *Shellfish that are gaping open* and do not close when tapped are dead. Throw out.
  - ▶ *If shells are closed completely* – up to seven days. This includes oysters, littlenecks, butter clams and cockles.
  - ▶ *If shells are not closed completely* – up to three to four days. This includes horse clams, softshell clams, geoducks and razor clams.
  - ▶ *Mussels* – up to three to four days.
  - ▶ *Shucked shellfish* (removed from their shells) – up to three days in refrigerator. Up to three months in freezer.
  - ▶ *Cooked shellfish* – up to two days in refrigerator. Up to three months in freezer.
  - ▶ *Thawed shellfish* taken from the freezer and thawed in a refrigerator – up to two days. Shellfish previously frozen and thawed should not be refrozen.

8. Know how to cook your shellfish. Shellfish may be prepared many ways. The Island County Health Department offers the following advice. If you have further questions please contact the county or state health departments:

- ✦ **Use small pots** when boiling or steaming shellfish. Cooking too many in one pot may prevent those in the middle from getting cooked thoroughly.
- ✦ **Discard any bivalve shellfish** – clams, oysters or mussels – that do not open.
- ✦ **Boil live bivalve shellfish** in water for 3-5 minutes or steam them in a preheated steamer for 4-9 minutes after the shell opens. **Bake live oysters** in the shell at least 10 minutes at 450° F. **Cook shucked oysters** for at least three minutes. You may boil or simmer them, or fry them in 375° F oil. If broiling, set the oysters three inches from the heat.
- ✦ **Cook shrimp** for 8 minutes once the water has returned to a full boil.

- **Clean crab** before cooking and eat only the meat. Crab can concentrate biotoxins such as Paralytic Shellfish Poison in their internal organs.
- **Cook crab** a minimum of 15 minutes once the water has returned to a full boil.

PUBLIC CLAMMING BEACHES

WDFW lists 56 Island County beaches with shellfish habitat. Many are tide-lands publicly accessible only by boat, which we don't include. For a clickable map of these and other public shellfish beaches, visit the WDFW website, www.wdfw.wa.gov/fish/shelfish/beachreg/. It shows current seasons for each, plus GPS coordinates for the boat-approached tidelands.

The list below shows sites in this book from which the public can walk to a potential clamming beach. Because biotoxin or pollution events can cause sudden changes, always confirm current status of any site. Call the hotlines above, or go to the Recreational Shellfish Program on the state Department of Health (DOH) website, www.doh.wa.gov/ehp/sf/recshell.htm, for clickable maps giving health status of each beach. From there, cross-click to harvesting information for the same beach on the WDFW interactive map. In some cases the DOH may list a beach as OPEN, meaning the clams are safe to eat, but it may be CLOSED to harvesting by WDFW due to resource depletion. Annual sport fishing pamphlet seasons are in effect for all beaches. For emergency regulation changes call WDFW's toll-free shellfish hotline, 1-866-880-5431.

Beach names used by DOH and WDFW are shown in brackets if they differ from our site names. Note some sites are permanently closed due to proximity to a sewage treatment plant, marina or ferry dock. Sites marked with Pollution Closure are currently closed due to bacteria levels. Some beaches have limited seasons. Check the WDFW *Fishing in Washington Guide Rule Pamphlet* for current status.

Site No.	Site Name
1, 3, 4	Deception Pass State Park sites
5	Ala Spit [Ala Spit & Ala Spit CP] *Limited season*
7	Dugualla Bay Dike [DNR-145]
8	Dugualla State Park [DNR-144] CLOSED *due to pollution*
11-14	Oak Harbor waterfront
	CLOSED (*marina and sewage plant outfall*)
18	Hastie Lake [North Point Partridge]
19	Monroe Landing CLOSED (*sewage plant outfall*)

Site No.	Site Name
20	Libbey Park [North Point Partridge]
21	Fort Ebey State Park
22	Grasser's Lagoon [West (North) Penn Cove]
23	West Penn Cove [West (North) Penn Cove & Madrona]
24-26	Coupeville waterfront *CLOSED (sewage plant outfall)*
27	Long Point *CLOSED to west – nearby sewage outfall*
29	Fort Casey State Park
31	Keystone Spit [South Fort Casey]
34	Hidden Beach [North Bluff]
37	South Whidbey State Park
41	Freeland County Park *CLOSED due to pollution*
44	Double Bluff [Useless Bay SP]
46	Sunlight Beach Access
49-50	Langley waterfront *CLOSED (sewage plant outfall)*
52	Dave Mackie Park *CLOSED due to pollution*
56	Possession Point State Park
64	Cavalero Park [Cavelaro (sic) Beach]
65	Cama Beach State Park *Limited or no season*
66	Camano Island State Park *Limited or no season*

© Robert Barnes

Digging for geoduck

Watch birds in all their specialized diversity

WHIDBEY ISLAND

Editor's note: Our thanks to Whidbey Audubon Society for this information. Birders flock to Whidbey Island for its rich diversity of bird species. The species noted in this section are representative – this is not a complete list. Many loons, grebes, diving ducks and others are present from fall through early spring. Some species such as warblers and swallows are found here spring through summer, while still others reside year round. Complete island bird lists are available at local libraries and many inns and B&Bs, and on the website of Whidbey Audubon, www. whidbeyaudubon.com Whidbey Audubon Society, P.O. Box 1012, Oak Harbor, WA 98277 or e-mail audubon@whidbey.com.

Female belted kingfisher

Killdeer

Both photographs © Craig Johnson

Deception Pass (Sites 1-4)

Turn west off Hwy 20 into state park opposite Cornet Bay Rd for rocky sandy shore, tide pools, fresh water wetland and rare beach plants. Turn east onto Cornet Bay Rd for waterfowl in Cornet Bay and forest birds in old growth forest at Hoypus Point. Good for loons, murrelets, oystercatcher, bald eagle, kingfisher, warblers, other passerines. A unique phenomenon occurs in winter, when red-throated loons from throughout the region gather to feed at the maximum outflow from Deception Pass. During the months of December to March, forty-five minutes to one hour before scheduled high tide at Port Townsend, watch from North Beach as hundreds of red-throated loons, as well as Pacific and common loons, cormorants, mergansers, pigeon guillemots and gulls, feed in the current flowing out through Deception Pass. The loons gather in long lines offshore, then fly in to feed, drifting out and returning, until, sated, they once again gather in long lines offshore before dispersing.

Dugualla Bay Dike (Site 7)

Water behind the dike and sheltered Dugualla Bay offer a mix of salt and fresh water, mudflats, and farm fields. Look for ducks, great blue heron, peregrine falcon, osprey, kingfisher and trumpeter swan. Best place on Whidbey to find canvasbacks.

Oak Harbor (Sites 11-14)

Oak Harbor beach and bay offer abundant waterfowl (including an occasional Eurasian wigeon), great blue heron, gulls (mew, ring-billed, Thayer's and others) and cormorants. In winter, flocks of black turnstones often hang around the marina (Site 11), and picnic nooks along the west end of the marina docks offer a close-up look at grebes and other water birds.

Joseph Whidbey State Park/Swan Lake/West Beach (Sites 16-17)

In the state park look for sandy beach, backshore, cattail marsh and forest birds, including savannah sparrow, Virginia rail, marsh wren, warblers and bald eagle. Swan Lake to the south offers a wide variety of waterfowl including ruddy duck, long-tailed duck, shoveler, wigeon, gadwall, bufflehead, coot and geese; sandpipers, yellowlegs and other shorebirds, and harriers. Feeding offshore may be loons, grebes, scoters, harlequin duck and pigeon guillemot.

Partridge Point (Hastie Lake, Site 18 and Libbey Park, Site 20)

Scan offshore for loons, grebes, pigeon guillemot and other alcids, harlequin duck, scoters, mergansers and other waterfowl. Black oystercatcher and whimbrel may be seen on the rocky beach below and sparrows and wrens in the brush.

Fort Ebey State Park (Site 21)

Habitats here include second growth forest, thickets, lake and beach. Birds found include marbled murrelet, mergansers, other waterbirds, kingfisher and a great mix of forest species including owls, pileated woodpecker, kinglets, brown creeper, flycatchers and warblers. Enjoy native vegetation and wildflowers along the bluff trails and beach.

West Penn Cove (Sites 22-23)

Park at Grasser's Lagoon turnout just southwest of Zylstra Rd or turn south from Hwy 20 onto Madrona Way. On the waters of Penn Cove and in the sheltered lagoons north and west of the cove may be seen abundant waterbirds such as common and red-throated loons, western and other grebes, cormorants, goldeneyes, scoters, bufflehead, and hooded merganser. In winter look on the rocky beaches for shorebirds including black turnstone, surfbird and sanderling.

Coupeville Wharf and Captain Coupe Park (Sites 25-26)

Salt water birds feeding here from fall to spring include loons, grebes, cormorants, gulls, common and Barrow's goldeneyes, scaups, all three species of scoters, bufflehead, great blue heron, kingfisher, and bald eagle. In summer look for pigeon guillemots and kingfishers nesting in holes in the bluff to the west.

Ebey's Landing/Bluff Trail/Perego Lagoon (Site 28)

Trails along bluff and beach offer rare prairie flowers, fields, thickets, forest, backshore lagoon, rocky beach, kelp beds and offshore waters. Birds seen include mourning dove, great horned owl, red-breasted nuthatch, chickadees, kinglets, warblers, finches; yellowlegs, killdeer, cormorants, grebes, mergansers, scoters, long-tailed duck, eagles and ravens.

Fort Casey State Park (Sites 29 and 30)

Along the rocky beach look for grebes, common and red-throated loons, harlequin duck, rhinocerous auklet, marbled murrelet, pigeon guillemot, Heerman's and other gulls and additional water birds. Thickets and forest harbor a wealth of woodpeckers, warblers, wrens, sparrows, other passerines and great horned owl.

Crockett Lake (Site 31)

This 250-acre brackish marsh and shallow lake is a foraging stopover during spring and fall migrations for large numbers of shorebirds including dowitchers, dunlin, western sandpiper, black-bellied and semi-palmated plovers, and avocet. Waterfowl include pintail, green-winged teal, shoveler, hooded merganser and Virginia rail. Raptors seen here include peregrine falcon, merlin, northern harrier, bald eagle, short-eared owl and an occasional snowy owl. A bird observation platform is located toward the east end of Keystone Spit (see figure p. 51), and is wheelchair-accessible.

South Whidbey State Park (Site 37)

The trail system at this park winds through old growth forest (ancient cedars and firs), home to woodpeckers, Steller's jay, thrushes, western tanager, violet-green swallow, winter wren, small perching birds (chickadees, brown creeper, nuthatch, etc.) and nesting osprey.

Double Bluff Beach and Deer Lagoon (Sites 44 and 45)

The sandy beach with high bluff offers viewing of gulls, waterfowl and bald eagle. Near the end of the road is a great blue heron rookery on the west hillside; watch from the road but do not disturb. To look over the marsh in Deer Lagoon, park on shoulder off the east side of Double Bluff road, or walk onto the dike from Sunlight Beach (Site 46).

Lone Lake (Site 47)
Look for birds of lake, woodlot, and thickets. You might see mergansers, shoveler, scaup, coot, other waterfowl; Steller's jay, bushtit, thrushes, yellow and other warblers; and quail.

Langley Seawall Park & Harbor (Sites 49-50)
Birds seen in these salt water and thicket habitats include cormorants, grebes, mergansers, loons, other waterfowl; bald eagle and small perching birds.

CAMANO ISLAND & STANWOOD

Editor's note: Our thanks to Pam Pritzl and the Camano Wildlife Habitat Project/Friends of Camano Island Parks for sharing this information. To learn more about birds in the Camano/Stanwood area contact Friends of Camano Island Parks, P.O. Box 1385, Stanwood, WA 98292 or go to www.whidbey.net/camparks/. Area birding field trips are also offered by Pilchuck Audubon Society, 1803 Hewitt Ave. #108, Everett, WA 98201, 425-252-0926, www.pilchuck-audubon.org or Skagit Audubon Society, P.O. Box 1101, Mount Vernon, WA 98273, www.fidalgo.net/~audubon/.

Camano Island

Livingston Bay (Site 62): Best at high tide in early morning or late afternoon, especially for ducks. When extensive mudflats form at low tide look for shorebirds.

English Boom Historical Preserve (Site 52): Excellent year round. Look for raptors, loons, scoters, ducks, great blue heron, shorebirds in migration, passerines and nesting purple martins (in summer). Bald eagle and osprey nest here. At low tide, seals haul out on exposed sand banks.

Utsalady Beach (Site 59): Good for deep-water birds such as loons, scoters and goldeneyes.

Maple Grove Park (Site 61): Saratoga Passage is at its narrowest here and the deep channel is close to shore. Loons, harlequin duck, cormorants, grebes and alcids (pigeon guillemot, marbled murrelet, rhinocerous auklet) are possible.

Kristoferson Beaver Marsh (Map p. 151): On Can Ku Rd across from the animal shelter, take the short trail to a platform to look out over the beaver marsh. Good for passerines and hooded merganser.

Iverson Spit Preserve (Site 63): Iverson Spit Preserve's diverse habitat includes extensive salt water, mudflats, marsh and beach, with shrub and cropland nestled against a forested hillside, providing the richest birding area on Camano Island. Over 140 species of birds have been seen here. Iverson Spit Preserve is on the Great Washington Birding Trail – Cascade Loop map (WWW.wa.audubon.org). River otter and coyote are seen regularly.

Four Springs Lake Preserve (Map p. 152): This 50-acre preserve consists of a mixed coniferous-deciduous forest with a lake and extensive wetlands. A one-mile perimeter trail is available for public use. Bald eagle, pileated wood-pecker and wood duck are common sightings.

Cama Beach State Park (Site 65): This park, soon to open to the public, has similar habitat to Camano Island State Park.

Camano Island State Park (Site 67): The park has several hiking trails through diverse habitats, including mixed coniferous-deciduous forest, wet-land and along extensive salt water (Saratoga Passage). Bald eagle, harlequin duck, loons, pileated woodpecker and mixed flocks of chickadees, kinglets and creepers are common.

Stanwood

Big Ditch: Go north from Stanwood on Old Pacific Hwy (102nd Ave) 2.4 miles, then just before the railroad track turn W (left) onto gravel Big Ditch Access Road 0.6 mile to parking lot. WDFW Vehicle Use Permit required. Excellent for wintering raptors and snow geese. Snowy owls are occasional winter visitors.

Stanwood Mitigated Wetlands: Located west of Heritage Park on 92nd Ave NW. Good for ducks, great blue heron, raptors and eventually passerines as newly planted vegetation grows larger.

Stanwood Sewage Lagoon: From Hwy 532 in Stanwood turn S onto 98th Ave NW. In 225 feet turn L into entrance to Stanwood Waste Water Treat-ment Plant. Birders are welcome; please check in at office for permission. Gate open weekdays. Arrange weekend visits in advance (360-629-8041). The several ponds, accessed on foot, are excellent for fresh water ducks, gulls, shorebirds in migration, and passerines.

Thomle and Boe Roads: Located off Marine Dr south of Stanwood, on the Stillaguamish delta. The main attractions in winter are snow geese, shore-birds in fields and wintering raptors, as well as sparrows in the thickets along Thomle Rd.

Make your dog dance for joy

Dogs are a big part of the island lifestyle. They welcome visitors to shops, fetch sticks at the beach, keep a watchful eye on the farm and panhandle treats at the drive-up. They love a good time and give joy generously. Many an islander owes the better part of a daily fitness program to these canine best friends who make exercise so much fun.

So take your dog. Besides, if you're even thinking about it, your dog is already celebrating.

OFF-LEASH DOG PARKS

Island County offers five off-leash parks—all located on Whidbey—through a joint effort by FETCH! (Free Exercise Time for Canines and their Humans) and the county parks department. FETCH! provides poop bags, fencing supplies, kiosks, water and much more. As of this printing there are no off-leash dog parks on Camano Island.

Oak Harbor Off-leash Area, 501 Technical Dr, Oak Harbor.
From Hwy 20 turn north on Goldie Road for 1 mile, then east on Technical Dr. The fenced park, just over an acre in size, is on the right at the street's end.

Clover Valley Off-leash Area, 799 Ault Field Rd, Oak Harbor.
From Hwy 20 go west on Ault Field Rd approximately 1 mile. The entrance to this 3-acre, fully-fenced dog park is on the right, just past the intersection with Oak Harbor Rd, west of the Clover Park ball fields.

Patmore Pit, 530 Patmore Rd, Coupeville.
Patmore Pit is south of Coupeville, west of the Naval Air Station Outlying Field. From Hwy 20 turn onto Patmore Road. Take second road on left, a short lane with dog park entrance gate at the end. This large area encompasses 40 partially-fenced acres of open space and woods. A separate fenced agility area can be reached by following a path straight back from the parking area.

Double Bluff Beach Access, Park at the south end of Double Bluff Road; Site 44.
This site offers great beach walking. The off-leash area starts at the windsock, about 500 feet from the parking lot. *Note: Owners allowing their dogs to run off-leash before this point are subject to a $500 fine for violating the county leash law.* A dog-height drinking fountain and dog rinse station are provided next to the parking lot. Parking can be tight, especially on summer weekends. Please do not park illegally; you risk being towed. In this multi-use area, please respect the off-leash boundaries and please pick up after your dogs!

Marguerite Brons Memorial Park, 2837 Becker Rd, Clinton.
From Hwy 525 drive south on Bayview Road. The park entrance is on your
left in about ½ mile, a short distance past the cemetery. Follow gravel road
to parking area. This 13-acre park is completely fenced. A two-acre fenced
meadow play area includes a covered picnic shelter and water station. Two
gates lead to trails that crisscross the remaining wooded area.

Good citizenship will keep opportunities open

As the islands grow more crowded, courtesy and good citizenship by dog
owners grow steadily more important in keeping opportunities open to pets
and their owners, including dog parks. FETCH! asks dog owners to diligently
observe these practices:

+ Use plastic bags to clean up after your dog.
+ Keep your dog from digging holes.
+ Stop bothersome behavior immediately.
+ Keep your dog on-leash until in the designated area.
+ Be respectful of all users of the park
+ Spay or neuter your dog.

Contact FETCH! at 360-321-4049, www.fetchparks.org.

How and why to dispose of pet waste properly

The health reasons for cleaning up dog waste are not well understood by some
owners. Pet waste contributes significantly to bacteria in our fresh and marine
waters. Waste from meat-eating animals can carry diseases and parasites.
Island County requires pet owners to pick up pet feces deposited at the beach,
on the street, in your yard, on the trail, sidewalk, ditch, litter box – anywhere
your pooch decides to poop. Pick it up in a plastic bag, tie it off and put it in
the garbage. Do not put into your compost pile any waste from meat-eating
pets. Neither is flushing an option. Flushing pet waste and kitty litter can clog
your septic or sewer system and
cause major backups and failures.
Kitty litter forms a thick, sticky
mass that blocks passages and
will not wash away. Always use
rubber gloves or a shovel when
handling feces of any animal
and be sure to wash your hands
thoroughly when finished.

© Dan Pedersen

Explore our glacial and geologic history

This aerial LIDAR (Light Distance and Ranging) map strips away the tree cover and plainly reveals the Ice Age story. Glacially carved north-south bedforms and scars dominate Whidbey and Camano islands. Keep your eyes open as you travel the islands and you will catch glimpses of the big picture.

LIDAR measures the terrain accurately to within 30 centimeters vertically (less than a foot) and about 60 centimeters horizontally. GIS (Geographical Information System) technology displays the LIDAR data. Hill shading is added to create a realistic, three-dimensional relief map.

Ice meets a barrier at Deception Pass

About 20,000 years ago, during the last of three glacial advances, ice flowed south from the coastal mountains of British Columbia. This "Puget Lobe" of the Vashon Glacier spread into the Puget Sound lowlands and covered Whidbey and Camano islands to a depth of 3,000 to 5,000 feet. Solid bedrock in the Deception Pass area formed a protective barrier to some degree for the land mass behind it–Whidbey Island.

Once the glacier had blocked the available outflow to the Strait of Juan de Fuca, lakes formed in the Puget Sound basin. Sediment accumulated in these lakes, eventually to be washed away by meltwater from the advancing ice, which gouged the north-south troughs of Puget Sound.

Old shorelines still visible

With vast amounts of the world's ocean water tied up in ice sheets, sea level dropped several hundred feet. Offsetting this, the weight of the ice compressed the land below sea level, where it remained for thousands of years until the ice melted and the land rose. The result was the formation of new shorelines, time after time.

These new shorelines are preserved in the geologic record as upland terraces and remain clearly visible on the LIDAR map today in such areas as Livingston Bay on Camano Island, to the north of Oak Harbor on Whidbey, and around Penn Cove near Coupeville.

Those out-of-place boulders were dropped here

The Puget Lobe of Vashon Glacier carried huge boulders and broke off chunks of rock from nearby mountains such as Mt. Erie, north of Deception Pass on Fidalgo Island, later dropping these glacial erratics on beaches, and in fields and neighborhoods on the two islands and elsewhere around Puget Sound.

NE-SW scars are visible north of Oak Harbor

Two exceptions to the predominant north-south orientation of landforms on Whidbey and Camano islands are an area of NE-SW scarring north of Oak Harbor, and the east-west orientation of Penn Cove. These were formed after the Puget Lobe withdrew and ice from the Cascade mountain glaciers re-advanced down the Skagit River Valley and across central Whidbey.

Lake beds and kettles remain

When the ice retreated about 13,000 years ago it left giant lake beds on central Whidbey. Finer sediments and nutrients flowed into these lakes and settled on the bottom. As the land rose, these lake beds became three fertile prairies that now lie within Ebey's Landing National Historical Reserve. The nearby, pock-marked "Kettles" area consists of many glacial-melt depressions as deep as 200 feet, created when large blocks of ice that had been trapped within the soils at the foot of the receding glacier melted.

Mammoths and mastodons roamed here

During interglacial periods, the Puget lowlands provided habitat for mastodons and mammoths, the bones and tusks of which are found from time-to-time on the bluffs and beaches of Camano and Whidbey islands. On Whidbey, remnants of these giant mammals have been found near Maxwelton Beach and Scatchet Head. A nearly complete tusk was excavated in the 1960s from a cliff on Camano Island north of Cama Beach.

LIDAR map of Island County. This map was provided by Island County Public Works, a participant in the Puget Sound LIDAR Consortium (PSLC). PSLC is an informal group of local and federal agencies led by the National Aeronautics and Space Administration (NASA) and the US Geological Survey.

Discover new trails for hiking, biking and horseback riding

Trails on Whidbey and Camano islands offer special opportunities for scenic hiking, mountain biking and horseback riding. Some favorites are listed here. For directions and maps, turn to the pages referenced in the first column.

Page(s)	Scenic hiking	Forest hiking	Mountain biking	Horseback riding	Name
17, 21, 138-9	●	●	●	●	Deception Pass State Park
21		●			Ala Spit
24			●		Dugualla State Park
27-29, 140	●				Oak Harbor Waterfront & Heritage Oaks
32, 141	●	●	●		Joseph Whidbey State Park
39, 142	●	●	●		Fort Ebey State Park
142		●	●	●	Kettles Trails
47	●				Ebey's Landing bluff trail
49-51, 143	●	●	●		Fort Casey State Park
144	●	●	●	●	Greenbank Farm
59, 145	●	●			South Whidbey State Park
146		●	●	●	Saratoga Woods, north of Langley
147		●	●	●	Goss Lake Woods, west of Langley
66	●				Double Bluff Beach
78	●	●			Possession Point State Park
81	●				English Boom Historical Preserve
88, 150	●				Iverson Spit Preserve
151		●	●	●	Camano Ridge Preserve
152		●			Four Springs Lake Preserve
153		●			Elger Bay Preserve
154		●	●		Cross Island Trail
92, 155	●	●	●		Camano Island State Park

BARRIER-FREE TRAILS

Sand Dune Interpretive Trail, Deception Pass State Park (Site 1; map p. 138). A ¾-mile paved loop starts at the south end of the West Beach parking lot next to Cranberry Lake, just past the restrooms. Views of marsh, beach forest, grassy sand dunes, the San Juan Islands and Olympic mountains.

Oak Harbor Waterfront Trail (Sites 11-14; map p. 140)
A paved trail runs nearly all 1½ miles from the city marina to the west end of Windjammer Park. Detour on streets around the private section between Flintstone and Windjammer parks. Park at the sites listed or on the street.

Kettles Trail and Coupeville waterfront
From the intersection of Highway 20 and Main Street at Coupeville, the first two miles are paved. The trail starts by Coupeville Elementary School and runs west, paralleling Hwy 20, with views across prairie farmland to mountains and water. Park at the school or the park-and-ride lot on the east side of South Main St, or two miles west of Coupeville where the pavement ends.

Along the Coupeville waterfront, a paved trail runs eastward from Coupeville Wharf (Site 25), at the end of Alexander St, most of the way to Captain Coupe Park (Site 26).

Rhododendron County Park
An old chip-sealed road runs through the center of this forested park just south of Coupeville, at 20265 SR 20. From Hwy 20, approximately 1½ miles south of Coupeville or 1 mile north of Patmore Rd, watch for campground tent signs. Turn south down gravel lane to park entrance. The old road runs from the lane end to Patmore Rd and is open to non-motorized travel. Vehicles can also park off-road along Patmore at the south end of the trail.

Maxwelton Nature Preserve (Site 51)
A level woodland trail and boardwalk lead through a wetland to a streamside viewing platform. This is a peaceful place to enjoy native plants.

South Whidbey Intermediate School Trails (Map p. 148)
An unpaved, reasonably level, handicapped-accessible forest trail leads from the parking area to Lizard Loop and connects to two former logging roads.

English Boom Preserve (Site 58)
A new boardwalk adjoining two ADA parking spaces offers vistas of this rich estuary.

PRIVATE LANDS WITH PUBLIC TRAILS

Several nonprofit organizations offer hiking trails open to the public.

Au Sable Institute - Pacific Rim Campus (Smith Prairie Reserve),
180 Parker Road, Coupeville. Phone: 360-678-5586.
Website: www.ausable.org/au.pacificrim.cfm. Smith Prairie Reserve sits on
175 acres formerly used as a state game farm. Site includes a Douglas fir forest
at the north end, a remnant glacial outwash prairie, domestic fields converted
to non-native grasses, and a homestead with several buildings. Au Sable trails
are open for walking and horseback riding, but no motorized vehicles. Prairie
plants are rare and fragile. Please remain on trails.

    Directions: From Hwy 20 two miles S of Coupeville turn onto Parker
Rd. The Smith Prairie Campus will be on your R.

Meerkerk Rhododendron Gardens, 3531 Meerkerk Lane, Greenbank.
Phone: 360-678-1912. Website: www.meerkerkgardens.org. Not-for-profit
garden, 2 miles south of Greenbank, open daily 9 am - 4 pm. Admission: $5,
children under 16 free when accompanied by an adult. Ten acres of display
and educational gardens enveloped by woodlands with four miles of nature
trails. Pets permitted on leash on the nature trails only, not in the gardens.

    Directions: From Highway 525 two miles S of Greenbank turn E onto
Resort Rd. Go 0.5 mile, turn L on Meerkerk Lane and follow signs to parking.

Earth Sanctuary, Newman Road, Freeland.
Phone: 360- 321-5465. Website: www.earthsanctuary.org. Nature reserve
and meditation park just south of Freeland. Open daily during daylight. Admission: $7. No dogs, please. Forests and ponds, megalithic sacred sites and
eco-art, a labyrinth for walking, and a Native American medicine wheel.

    Directions: From Clinton, drive N on Hwy 525 about 7 miles. Turn R
onto Newman Rd for 0.8 mile to Earth Sanctuary sign on R side of the road,
with "2059" on the mailbox. Turn R into this driveway, bear R at the Y and
continue 100 feet to the parking lot.

Whidbey Institute, Campbell Road, Clinton.
Phone: 360-341-1884. Website: www.whidbeyinstitute.org. Public welcome
on trails of this 70-acre forest and meadow called the Chinook lands. No
dogs or other pets.

    Directions: From Hwy 525 two miles N of Clinton, turn W at stoplight
onto Cultus Bay Rd. Go about 0.5 mile, turn R onto Campbell Rd. In 0.2
mile, at signs for Whidbey Institute and Chinook, turn L onto gravel road.
Follow through forest. Trailhead parking and info kiosk are at bottom of hill
before driveway climbs uphill.

CHAPTER SIX

Trail Maps

Whidbey and Camano islands offer miles of trails for public use on shoreline, prairie and forest lands. They are maintained by state, national or county park systems, school districts and municipalities, or under the stewardship of private, non-profit organizations. Please treat these trails with respect, observe any rules, clean up after your pets and pick up any litter.

Editor's note: We drafted these maps from public domain sources or from copyright sources with permission of the copyright holder. When the source map had a scale reference, we included it. Scale varies from map to map. We cannot guarantee accuracy.

KEY TO MAPS

Trails

-- Hikers only
-·- Hikers and mountain bikes
·-· Hikers and horses only
····· Hikers, mountain bikes and horses

Point of interest

65 Corresponds with site number in Chapter 3
P Parking area
  Dock or pier
  Boat ramp
  Flush toilet
  Portable or vault toilet
  Campground
K Information kiosk
  Barrier-free (handicapped accessible) trail
  Picnic table(s)
  Picnic shelter(s)
  Playground
  Ranger station
  Fishing

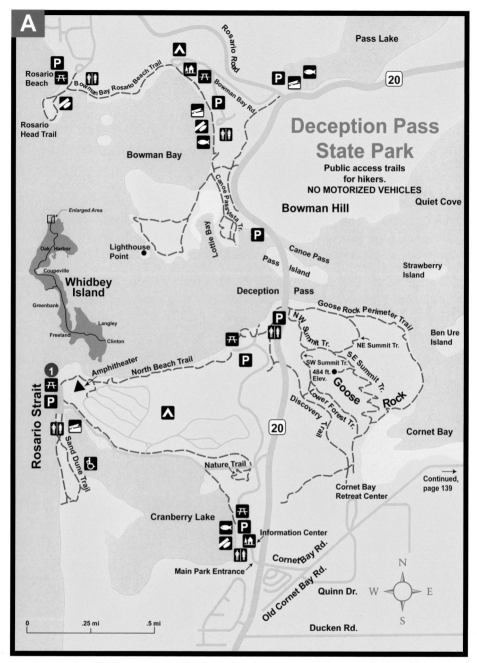

A

Pass Lake

Rosario Road

Rosario Beach

Bowman Bay Rosario Beach Trail

Bowman Bay Rd.

20

Rosario Head Trail

Bowman Bay

Deception Pass State Park

Public access trails for hikers.
NO MOTORIZED VEHICLES

Bowman Hill

Quiet Cove

Canoe Pass Vista Tr.

Enlarged Area

Lighthouse Point

Oak Harbor

Lottie Bay

Canoe Pass

Coupeville

Pass Island

Strawberry Island

Whidbey Island

Greenbank

Langley

Deception Pass

Goose Rock Perimeter Trail

Freeland

Clinton

Ben Ure Island

NW Summit Tr.

NE Summit Tr.

Amphitheater

North Beach Trail

SW Summit Tr.

SE Summit Tr.

Rosario Strait

484 ft.
Elev.

Goose Rock

1

Lower Forest Tr.

Sand Dune Trail

Discovery Trail

20

Cornet Bay

Nature Trail

Continued, page 139

Cornet Bay Retreat Center

Cranberry Lake

Information Center

Main Park Entrance

Cornet Bay Rd.

Old Cornet Bay Rd.

N

W ⊕ E

Quinn Dr.

S

0   .25 mi   .5 mi

Ducken Rd.

Some park trails are near steep banks and cliffs, so be sure to carefully attend children. (See page 17.)

GREEN
TRAILS
MAPS™

One of the ten essentials
www.greentrailsmaps.com

By permission:
Green Trails Maps ™
DECEPTION PASS
Anacortes Community
Forest lands (ACFL) Map 41S

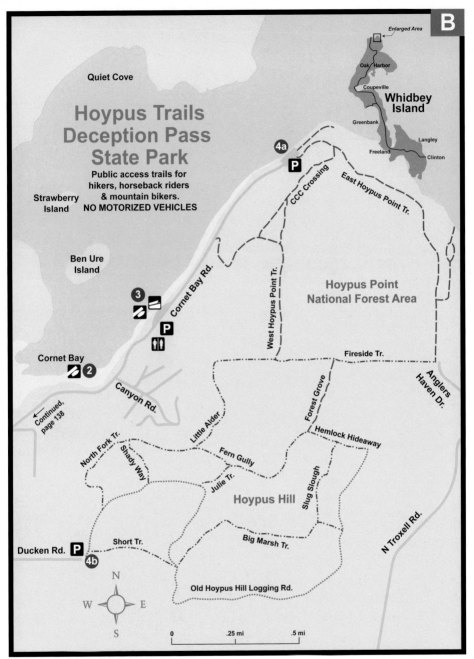

B

Quiet Cove

Hoypus Trails
Deception Pass
State Park

Public access trails for
hikers, horseback riders
& mountain bikers.
NO MOTORIZED VEHICLES

Strawberry
Island

Ben Ure
Island

Enlarged Area

Oak Harbor

Coupeville

**Whidbey
Island**

Greenbank

Langley

Freeland

Clinton

CCC Crossing

East Hoypus Point Tr.

4a

P

West Hoypus Point Tr.

Cornet Bay Rd.

**Hoypus Point
National Forest Area**

3

P

Cornet Bay

2

Canyon Rd.

Fireside Tr.

Anglers Haven Dr.

Continued,
page 138

North Fork Tr.

Shady Way

Little Alder

Fern Gully

Julie Tr.

Forest Grove

Hemlock Hideaway

Slug Slough

Hoypus Hill

Ducken Rd. P

4b

Short Tr.

Big Marsh Tr.

N Troxell Rd.

N

W   E

S

Old Hoypus Hill Logging Rd.

0   .25 mi   .5 mi

Use Cornet Bay Rd trailheads for Hoypus Point Natural Forest Area (walkers only), and take
Ducken Rd to Hoypus Hill trailhead for walkers, horses and mountain bikes. (See page 21.)

GREEN
TRAILS
MAPS™

One of the ten essentials

www.greentrailsmaps.com

By permission:
Green Trails Maps ™
DECEPTION PASS
Anacortes Community
Forest lands (ACFL) Map 41S

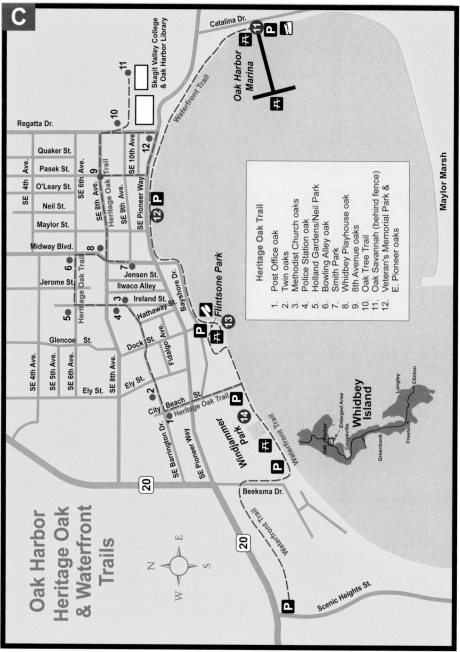

C

Oak Harbor
Heritage Oak
& Waterfront
Trails

Catalina Dr.

Oak Harbor Marina

Skagit Valley College & Oak Harbor Library

Waterfront Trail

Regatta Dr.

Quaker St.
Pasek St.
O'Leary St.
Neil St.
Maylor St.
Midway Blvd.

SE 4th Ave.
SE 6th Ave.
SE 8th Ave.
SE 9th Ave.
SE 10th Ave.
SE Pioneer Way
Heritage Oak Trail

Jerome St.
Jensen St.
Ilwaco Alley
Ireland St.
Hathaway St.
Glencoe St.

SE 4th Ave.
SE 5th Ave.
SE 6th Ave.
SE 8th Ave.
Heritage Oak Trail

Dock St.
Ely St.
City Beach St.
Heritage Oak Trail

SE Barrington Dr.
SE Pioneer Way

Fidalgo Ave.
Bayshore Dr.

Flintsone Park

Windjammer Park

Beeksma Dr.

Scenic Heights St.

Waterfront Trail

20

Maylor Marsh

Whidbey Island

Oak Harbor
Coupeville
Greenbank
Freeland
Langley
Clinton

Enlarged Area

N
E
S
W

Heritage Oak Trail

1. Post Office oak
2. Twin oaks
3. Methodist Church oaks
4. Police Station oak
5. Holland Gardens/Neil Park
6. Bowling Alley oak
7. Smith Park
8. Whidbey Playhouse oak
9. 8th Avenue oaks
10. Oak Tree Trail
11. Oak Savannah (behind fence)
12. Veteran's Memorial Park &
    E. Pioneer oaks

For a walking tour of the Oak Harbor's namesake trees, follow the dotted line. Many of these heritage oaks are estimated between 150 and 300 years old. The Garry oak was once common on dry, open sites from British Columbia to California, forming a distinct meadow ecosystem with camas, shooting star, and other native plants and grasses. Glimpse a fenced remnant of oak savannah on Navy property behind Skagit Valley College (Stop #11).

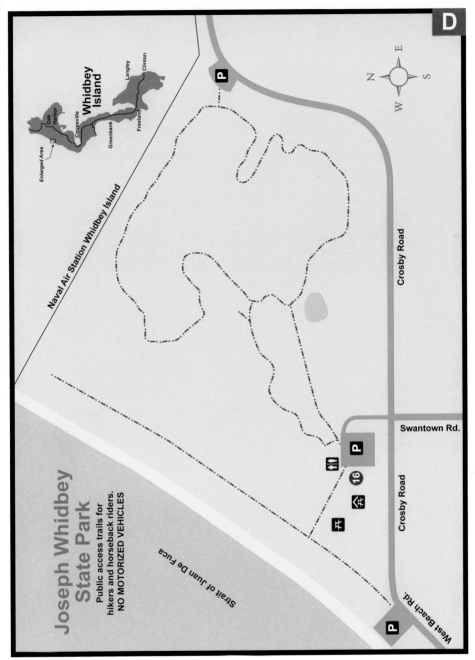

From Oak Harbor take Swantown Rd to Crosby Rd. (See page 32.)

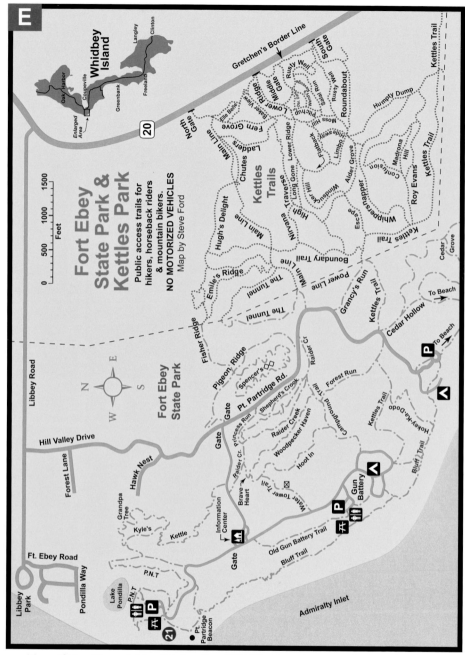

Turn off Hwy 20 onto Libbey Rd, then S on Hill Valley Dr to the state park. Limited parking is available at the Kettles Trail entrances along Hwy 20, on the hill S of Libbey Rd at gates signed, "Non-motorized Trail." (See page 39.)

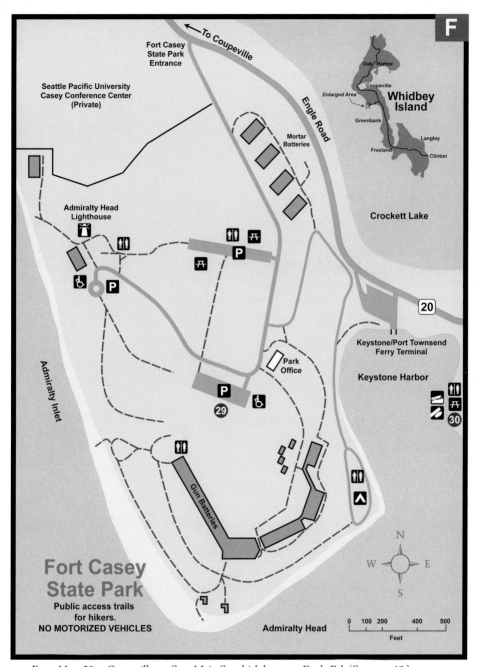

From Hwy 20 at Coupeville, go S on Main St, which becomes Engle Rd. (See page 49.)

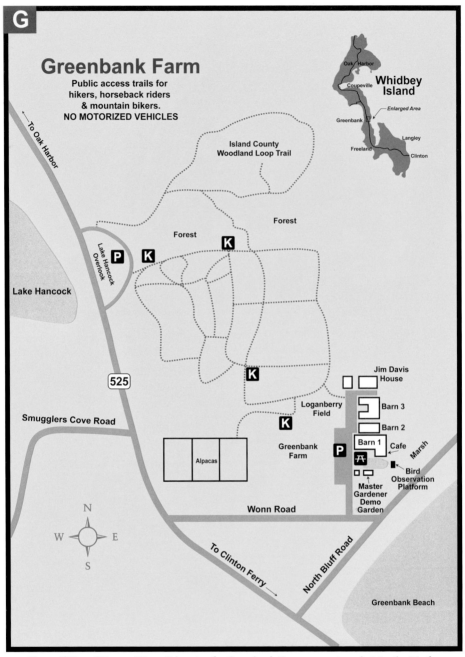

Turn off Hwy 525 onto Wonn Rd at sign for Greenbank Farm, approximately 14 miles N of Clinton, 10 miles S of Coupeville.

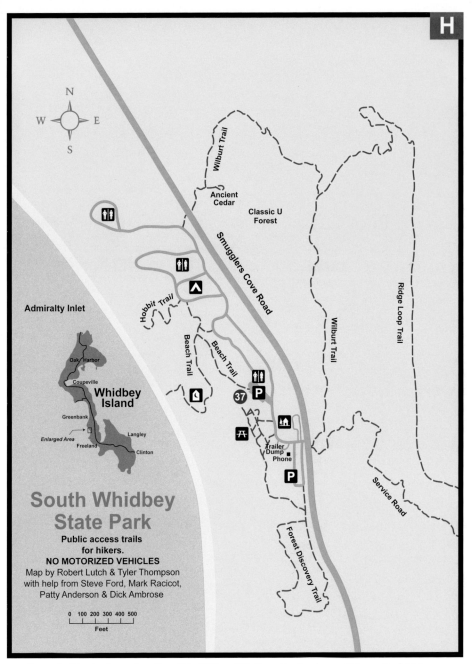

From the N, take Smugglers Cove Rd off Hwy 525. From Freeland, turn W onto Bush Point Rd, which becomes Smugglers Cove Rd. (See page 59.)

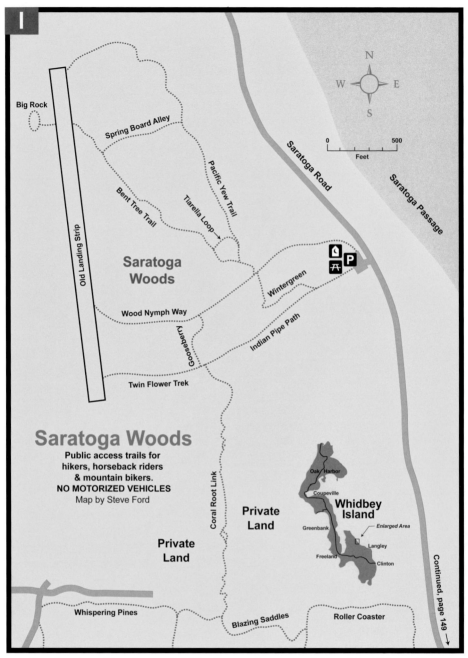

Continued, page 149 →

From Langley go N on Saratoga Rd 2.5 miles to parking area on L. From Hwy 525, turn N at traffic light onto Bayview Rd. Travel approximately 3 miles to DeBruyn Ave, turn L to stop sign, then L on Saratoga Rd and follow directions above.

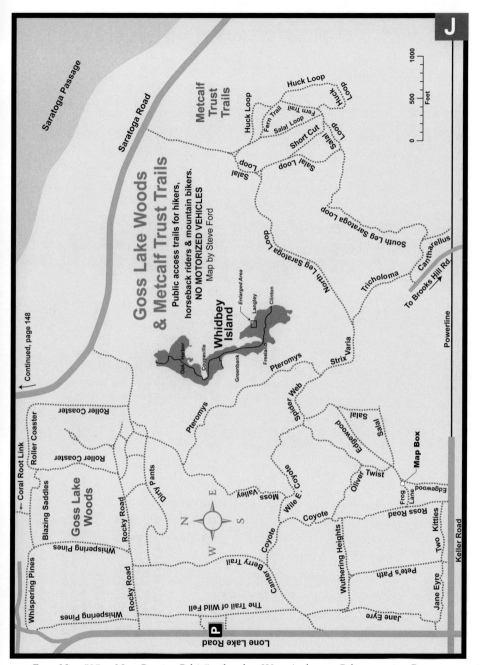

Goss Lake Woods & Metcalf Trust Trails

Public access trails for hikers, horseback riders & mountain bikers.
NO MOTORIZED VEHICLES
Map by Steve Ford

Metcalf Trust Trails

Whidbey Island

Goss Lake Woods

← Continued, page 148

From Hwy 525 go N on Bayview Rd 1.5 miles, then W on Andreason Rd to stop sign, R on Lone Lake Rd. Parking area is ½-mile N of Keller Rd.

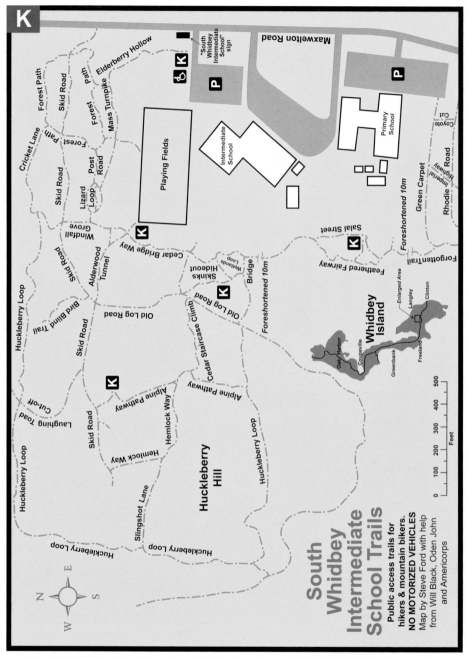

From Hwy 525, go N on Maxwelton Rd 0.9 mile to sign on L for South Whidbey Intermediate School, the last of four driveways serving the Primary and Intermediate schools. Park on N side of driveway next to kiosk or in school lots outside school hours. Trails are open to the public on weekends and weekdays when school is not in session. During the school day, please register with the office.

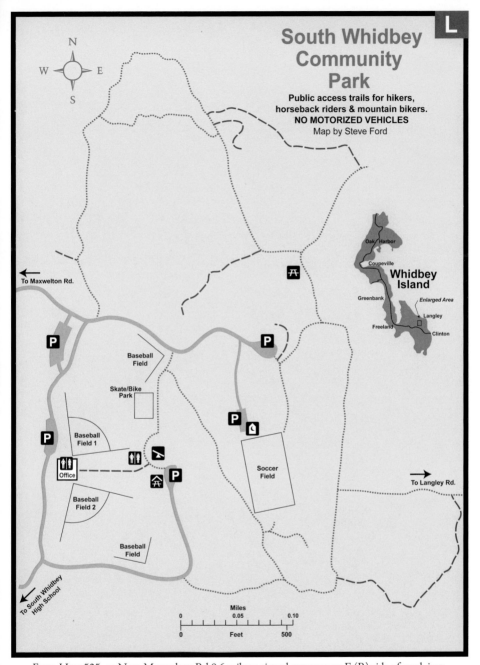

South Whidbey Community Park

Public access trails for hikers, horseback riders & mountain bikers.
NO MOTORIZED VEHICLES
Map by Steve Ford

L

N
W E
S

To Maxwelton Rd.

Baseball Field

Skate/Bike Park

Baseball Field 1

P

Office

Baseball Field 2

Baseball Field

Soccer Field

To Langley Rd.

To South Whidbey High School

Whidbey Island

Oak Harbor
Coupeville
Greenbank
Enlarged Area
Langley
Freeland
Clinton

Miles
0   0.05   0.10
0   Feet   500

From Hwy 525, go N on Maxwelton Rd 0.6 mile to signed entrance on E (R) side of road, just N of South Whidbey High School.

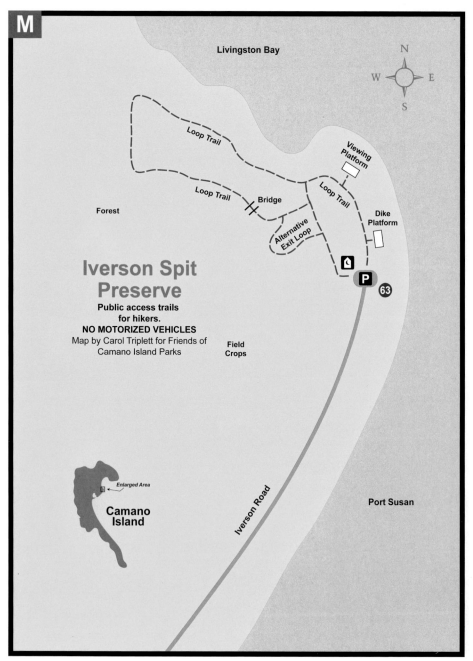

M

Livingston Bay

N
W — E
S

Loop Trail

Viewing
Platform

Loop Trail

Bridge

Loop Trail

Dike
Platform

Forest

Alternative
Exit Loop

P 63

Iverson Spit
Preserve

**Public access trails
for hikers.
NO MOTORIZED VEHICLES**
Map by Carol Triplett for Friends of
Camano Island Parks

Field
Crops

Enlarged Area

**Camano
Island**

Iverson Road

Port Susan

From Hwy 532, S on Sunrise Rd. Turn L on Iverson Rd and head E and N to
parking area at the end. (See page 88.)

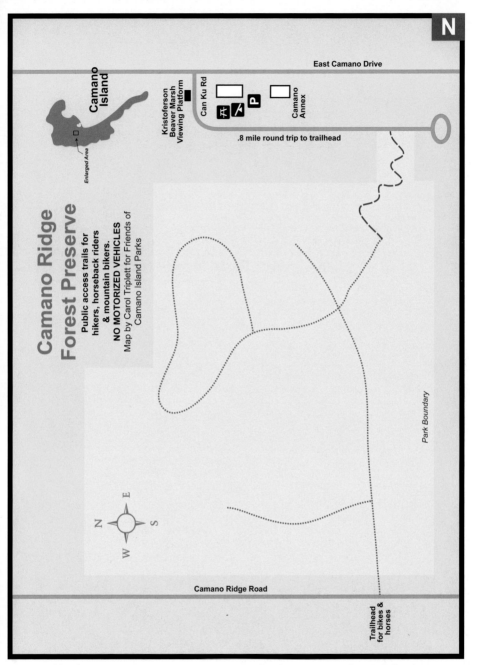

East Camano Drive

Camano Island

Can Ku Rd

Kristoferson
Beaver Marsh
Viewing Platform

P

Camano
Annex

.8 mile round trip to trailhead

Enlarged Area

**Camano Ridge
Forest Preserve**

Public access trails for
hikers, horseback riders
& mountain bikers.
NO MOTORIZED VEHICLES
Map by Carol Triplett for Friends of
Camano Island Parks

N
W   E
S

Park Boundary

Camano Ridge Road

Trailhead
for bikes &
horses

From Terry's Corner go S on East Camano Dr 2.1 miles. On R, just past Can Ku Rd, is 6 acre complex of Camano Annex and public park with tennis court, ballfield, playground, picnic area and multi-purpose center. Park here and walk ½ mile up Can Ku Rd to Camano Ridge trailhead. Visit Kristoferson Beaver Marsh viewing platform on the way. There is limited on-street parking at trailhead. Bicyclists and horse riders must enter from the west gate on Camano Ridge Rd, just N of Carp Lake Rd.

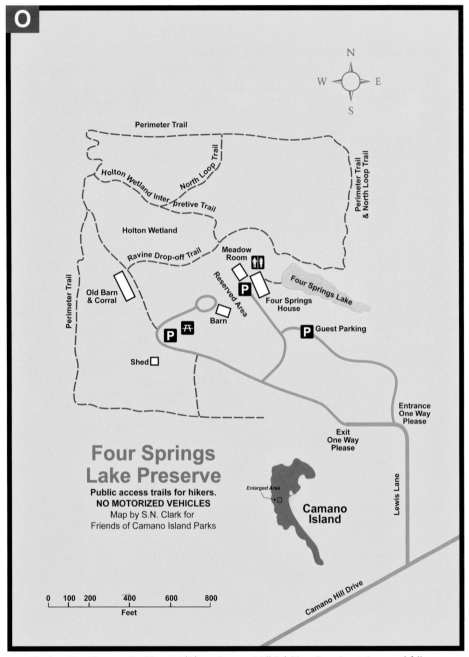

Four Springs Lake Preserve

Public access trails for hikers.
NO MOTORIZED VEHICLES
Map by S.N. Clark for
Friends of Camano Island Parks

Go S on East Camano Dr. Turn W (R) on Camano Hill Rd. Turn R on Lewis Lane and follow one-way signs to Four Springs. Pass guest parking area and continue toward exit, then turn R on gravel road to picnic area parking for trailhead.

In 2001 Island County purchased the land with Conservation Futures funds, and the buildings with the help of Friends of Camano Island Parks. Trails are open to the public for day use. The buildings are available for day use rental. Phone 360-387-1418 or www.fourspringshouse.com.

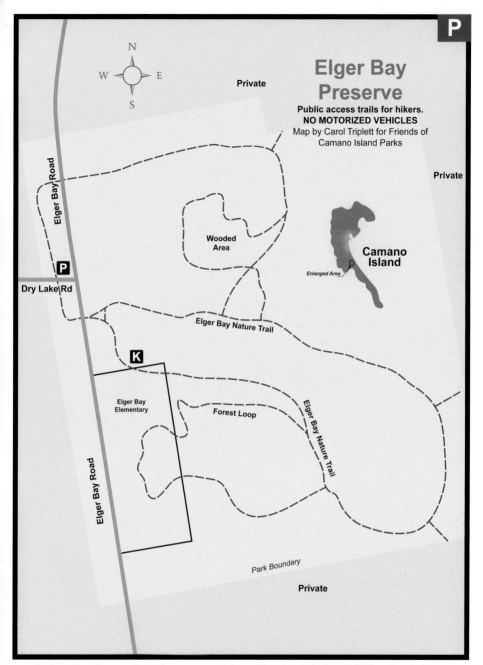

Go S on East Camano Dr and continue straight on Elger Bay Rd. Turn R (W) on Dry Lake Rd and park immediately on the R or L shoulders. Dry Lake Rd is 0.5-mile N of Elger Bay Store. Follow designated trail N or S to crossings, to trailheads on E side of Elger Bay Rd.

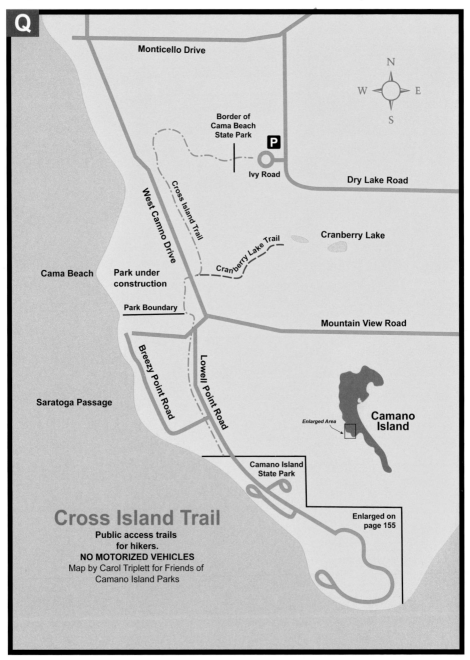

Q

Monticello Drive

Border of
Cama Beach
State Park

P

Ivy Road

Dry Lake Road

West Camno Drive

Cross Island Trail

Cranberry Lake Trail

Cranberry Lake

Cama Beach

Park under
construction

Park Boundary

Mountain View Road

Breezy Point Road

Lowell Point Road

Saratoga Passage

Enlarged Area

Camano
Island

Camano Island
State Park

Enlarged on
page 155

Cross Island Trail

**Public access trails
for hikers.
NO MOTORIZED VEHICLES**
Map by Carol Triplett for Friends of
Camano Island Parks

N
W · E
S

Go S on East Camano Dr and continue straight on Elger Bay Rd. Turn R (W) on Dry Lake Rd, about 0.5-mile N of Elger Bay Store. Go 1.4 miles to Ivy Rd trailhead. Please do not park in front of the mailboxes.

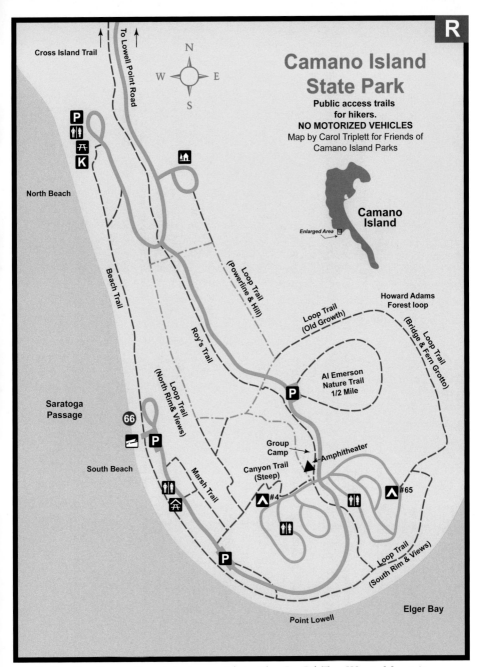

Camano Island State Park

Public access trails for hikers.
NO MOTORIZED VEHICLES
Map by Carol Triplett for Friends of Camano Island Parks

Camano Island

Enlarged Area

Go S on East Camano Dr and continue straight on Elger Bay Rd. Turn W onto Mountain View Rd, then S onto Lowell Point Rd to park entrance. (See page 92.)

Editor's note: Our Camano trail maps are based on the booklet, "Walking the Camano Island Trails," created and distributed by Friends of Camano Island Parks, PO Box 1385, Stanwood, WA 98292. Regularly updated, it includes additional maps and information beyond what is reproduced in this book.

TABLE OF SHORELINE ACCESSES

Section colors correspond with Chapter 3 divisions.

● Amenity or activity available.

▲ Barrier-free access to one or more features. May not meet ADA Guidelines.

Parking: 1, 2, etc. = Number of spaces. A = Multiple lots. B = No on-site parking, but nearby public parking. X = Closed at time of printing.

Accessible amenities: Triangle = reasonably barrier-free. Trails p. 134.

Amenities: Restroom (flush), pit/portable toilet, portable water, picnic tables, picnic shelters, barbecue/firepit and playground.

Dock/pier: Boat dock and/or fishing pier. Some docks removed seasonally.

Moorage: Boat moorage. Limitations may apply.

Boat ramp: Tides may limit. Some boat-trailer parking.

Hand-carry boat: Suitable to hand-carry kayaks, canoes, etc.

Beach walking: Connects with 600 feet or more of public tideland.

Swimming: Considered good for swimming.

Clams: Walking access to beach with shellfish habitat. Check shellfish safety and rule changes before digging. See pages 118-122. C = Closed to shellfish harvest due to pollution risk. D = Harvest season limited or closed due to resource depletion.

Fishing: Shore casting. WDFW permit and seasons apply.

Bird watching: More information pages 123-128. See page 117.

Trails: Upland trails. Maps for many, Chapter 6.

Parking vista: View from parking area.

WWT camp: Washington Water Trails campsite for those arriving by water in a non-motorized boat.

Ownership: CP=Town of Coupeville; DOD = US Department of Defense; EL = Washington State Parks, National Park Service, The Nature Conservancy and a Sherman-Bishop Farms easement; IC=Island County; LY = City of Langley; OH = City of Oak Harbor; PC = Port of Coupeville; PSW = Port of South Whidbey; PSWIC = Port of South Whidbey & Island County; SP = Washington State Parks; SWSD = South Whidbey School District; WDFW = Washington Department of Fish & Wildlife (Vehicle Use Permit required).

Length of public beach (linear feet): Estimated length of public tideland reachable from the access before encountering private tideland. None = no tideland.

Site #	Site Name	Parking	Accessible amenities	Restroom (flush)	Pit/portable toilet	Drinking water	Picnic tables	Picnic shelters	Barbecue/firepit	Playground	Dock/pier	Moorage	Boat ramp	Hand-carry boat	Beach walking	Swimming	Clams	Fishing	Bird watching	Trails	Parking vista	WWT camp	Ownership	Length of public beach (feet)
1	Deception Pass State Park	A	▲	▲		•	▲	•	•					•	•	•	•	•	•		•	•	SP	73,920
2	Cornet Bay County Dock	10									•	•		•				•	•				IC	50
3	Cornet Bay Boat Launch	110	▲	▲		•	•				▲	•	•	•				•	•				SP	12,075
4	Hoypus Point	8,6												•	•				•	•	•		SP	12,075
5	Ala Spit	10-15			•									•	•				•	•	•	•	IC	1,800
6	Moran Beach	10-15												•	•				•	•			IC	100
7	Dugualla Bay Dike Access	5												•					•		•		IC	7,900
8	Dugualla State Park	4												•	•		C					SP	6,690
9	Borgman Road End	2												•	•				•	•			IC	40
10	Mariners Cove Boat Launch	4												•					•				IC	245
11	Oak Harbor City Marina	50+	▲	▲		•	•	•		•	▲	•	•	•	•		C	•	•	▲			OH	2,640
12	Pioneer Way East	B										•		•			C	•	•	▲			OH	644
13	Flintstone Park	B	▲	▲			•	•			•	•		•			C	•	•	▲			OH	415
14	Windjammer Park	100	▲	▲		•	•	•	•	•			•	•	•	•	C	•	•	▲	•		OH	2,380
15	Rocky Point Picnic Area	10+			•								•	•	•				•			•	DOD	2,640
16	Joseph Whidbey State Park	25+	▲		•	•			•					•	•				•	•	•	•	SP	3,100
17	West Beach Vista	12												•	•				•		•		IC	9,775
18	Hastie Lake Boat Launch	10											•	•	•				•		•		IC	26,400
19	Monroe Landing	8	▲	▲										•	•		C		•		•		IC	2,640
20	Libbey Beach Park	10	▲	▲		•	•	•	•					•	•			•	•	•			IC	42,240
21	Fort Ebey State Park	A		▲		•	•	•	•					•	•			•	•			•	SP	15,840
22	Grasser's Lagoon	8-10												•				•	•				WDFW	2,640

Site #	Site Name	Parking	Accessible amenities	Restroom (flush)	Pit/portable toilet	Drinking water	Picnic tables	Picnic shelters	Barbecue/firepit	Playground	Dock/pier	Moorage	Boat ramp	Hand-carry boat	Beach walking	Swimming	Clams	Fishing	Bird watching	Trails	Parking vista	WWT camp	Ownership	Length of public beach (feet)
23	West Penn Cove Access	6												●	●		●		●				WDFW	4,640
24	Coupeville Town Park	12	◀	◀		●	●	●	●	●					●		C						CP	2,640
25	Coupeville Wharf & Beach	B	◀	◀		●			●		●	●		●	●		C						PC	2,640
26	Captain Coupe Park	8	◀	◀		●	●				●		●	●	●		C		●		●	●	CP	8,536
27	Long Point	10-15													●	●	●	●	●		●		IC	13,135
28	Ebey's Landing	15+			◀										●			●	●	●	●		EL	21,120
29	Fort Casey State Park	A	◀	◀		◀	●	●	●					●	●		●	●	●	●	●		SP	10,800
30	Keystone Jetty	50+													●	●			●	●		●		SP	500
31	Keystone Spit	50+													●	●		●	●	●		●		SP	7,920
32	Driftwood Beach Park	20			●				●							●								IC	245
33	Ledgewood Beach Access	5-6														●		●						IC	13,200
34	Hidden Beach	X														●								IC	730
35	Lagoon Point North	10													●				●			●		IC	434
36	Lagoon Point South	2-3													●				●					IC	30
37	South Whidbey State Park	A	◀	◀		◀	●	●	●						●	●		●	●	●	●			SP	4,500
38	Bush Point Boat Launch	24	◀	◀							●		●	●				●					PSW	30,400
39	Bush Point-Sandpiper Rd	2-4											●	●				●					IC	45
40	Mutiny Bay Vista	7																				●		IC	295
41	Freeland Park	30+	◀	◀		●	●	●	●	●	●		●	●	●		C				●		PSWIC	2,020
42	Mutiny Bay Boat Launch	15+			●								●	●									PSWIC	60
43	Mutiny Bay Shores	1-2																	●					IC	950
44	Double Bluff Beach	20	◀												●	●		●		●		●		IC	10,560

Site #	Site Name	Parking	Accessible amenities	Restroom (flush)	Pit/portable toilet	Drinking water	Picnic tables	Picnic shelters	Barbecue/firepit	Playground	Dock/pier	Moorage	Boat ramp	Hand-carry boat	Beach walking	Swimming	Clams	Fishing	Bird watching	Trails	Parking vista	WWT camp	Ownership	Length of public beach (feet)
45	Deer Lagoon	1-2																	●				IC	None
46	Sunlight Beach Access	2																	●				IC	1,575
47	Lone Lake	20			●	●	●							●				●	●				IC	None
48	Goss Lake	8			●	●	●						●	●				●					IC	None
49	Langley Seawall Park	B	▲	●										●	●	●	C	●	●				LY	1000
50	Langley Boat Harbor & Pier	10	▲	●							●	●	●	●		●	C	●	●		●		LY	200
51	Maxwelton Nature Preserve	7	▲	▲									●							▲			SWSD	None
52	Dave Mackie Park	50	▲	▲											●		C		●		●		PSWIC	420
53	Deer Lake	6			●													●					IC	None
54	Clinton Beach and Pier	B	▲	▲		●	●	●	●	●	▲	●		●		●		●					PSW	179
55	Glendale Parking Access	2-3										●				●					●		IC	None
56	Possession Point State Park	10	▲	▲	●									●	●		●	●		●	●	●	SP	5,072
57	Possession Beach Park	30+	▲			●	●		●		●		●	●	●			●	●	●	●		PSW	677
58	English Boom Preserve	16			●			●							●				●	▲	●	●	IC	300
59	Utsalady Beach	10			●								●										IC	500
60	Utsalady Vista Park	3			●														●				IC	None
61	Maple Grove Park	10-12			●				●				●	●							●		IC	250
62	Livingston Bay	10-15												●					●				IC	90
63	Iverson Spit Preserve	5			●								●	●	●			●	●		●		IC	2,400
64	Cavalero Park and Boat Launch	15-20			●				●							●	D		●				IC	250
65	Cama Beach State Park	OPENING 2008							D	D													SP	5,280
66	Camano Island State Park	A	▲	▲	●	●	●	●	●				●	●	●	●	D	●	●		●	●	SP	6,800
67	Tillicum Beach	4																					IC	80

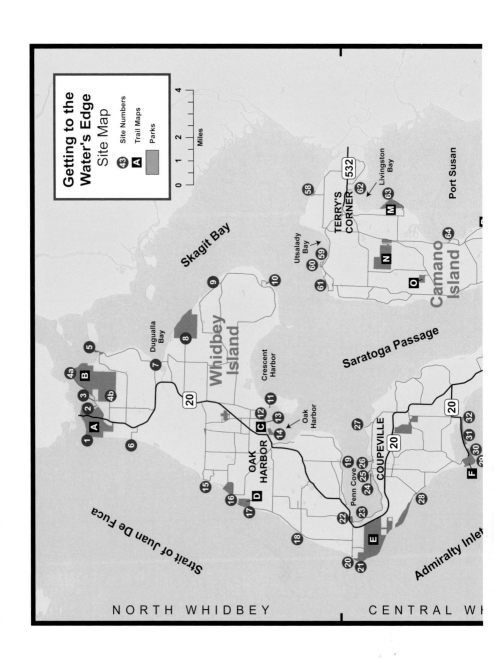

Getting to the Water's Edge
Site Map

43 Site Numbers
A Trail Maps
Parks

0 1 2 3 4
Miles

Skagit Bay

Dugualla Bay

Whidbey Island

Crescent Harbor

Oak Harbor

OAK HARBOR

Penn Cove

COUPEVILLE

Saratoga Passage

Strait of Juan De Fuca

Admiralty Inlet

TERRY'S CORNER

532

Livingston Bay

Utsalady Bay

Camano Island

Port Susan

NORTH WHIDBEY   CENTRAL WH

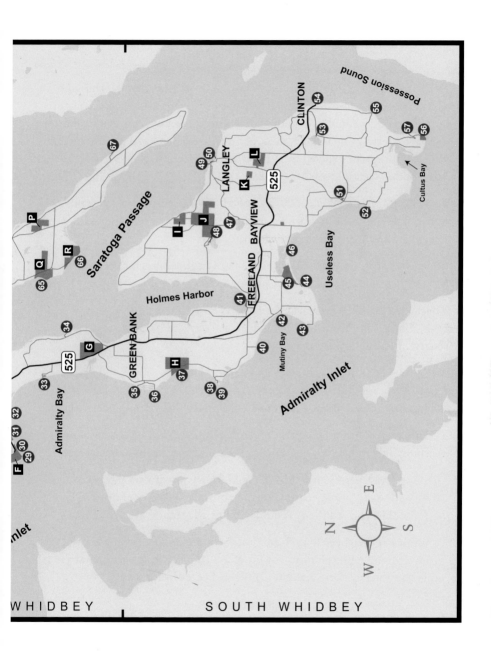

Where to learn more

Libraries and bookstores are filled with resources. The World Wide Web brings instant access to any search topic. Here are a few places to start – a taste of what's available.

If you're buying or building on the shoreline

Department of Ecology, www.ecy.wa.gov, click on "Shorelands." This large and informative website has important tips for anyone exploring, buying or building on the shoreline, including bulkhead alternatives, preventing erosion, drainage control, landscaping, rules, permits, shoreline aerial photos. Helpful publications can be ordered from the website or from Ecology's Publication Distribution Center, 360-407-7472.

Puget Sound Action Team, 800-547-6863, www.psat.wa.gov. Click on "Low Impact Development" to learn environmentally sensitive techniques for developing land and managing stormwater runoff.

Shore Stewards, www.shorestewards.org. Ten guidelines for shoreline living, links to free publications and website resources.

Terich, Thomas A., *Living with the Shore of Puget Sound and the Georgia Strait*, Duke University Press, 1987. A guide to geology and hazards along each stretch of Island County shoreline.

Ecology and natural history

Lamb, Andy and Bernard P. Hanby, *Marine Life of the Pacific Northwest: A Photographic Encyclopedia*, Harbour Publishing, 2005. Comprehensive guide.

Kozloff, Eugene N., *Seashore Life of the Northern Pacific Coast*, University of Washington Press, 1993. The classic on Pacific Northwest intertidal life.

Washington Department of Fish & Wildlife, www.wdfw.wa.gov. In addition to fish and shellfish information, this site includes a library of tips on "Living with Wildlife" and a "Fish & Wildlife Online Magazine."

WSU Beach Watchers, www.beachwatchers.wsu.edu. Click on "EZ-ID Guides" for an online guide to dozens of intertidal organisms, or purchase a laminated Intertidal Invertebrates ID Card Set for beach use.

Other resources

Snohomish Conservation District (serving Camano), www.snohomishcd.org
Whidbey Conservation District, www.whidbeycd.org
WSU Extension - Island County, www.island.wsu.edu

INDEX

Salmon Technical Advisory Group
(Salmon TAG), 12
sand dollars, 103-104, 109, 111
sand lance, see forage fish
Sandpiper Rd, see Bush Point
Sandy Point, 111
Saratoga Passage, 8-9, 18, 71-72,
92, 114, 116
Saratoga Woods, 133, 146
sea cucumbers, 50, 103, 110
sea stars, 20, 43, 50, 72, 99,
102-103, 109, 112
seals, seal pups, 7, 23, 31, 77, 82,
108-109, 111, 113, 126
seaweeds, 13, 34, 38, 104-105, 120
sediment transport, 25, 33, 49,
66, 67
septic systems, 10, 11, 62, 129
shellfish, 1-7, 28, 40, 44, 62,
118-121, 156, 162
Shore Stewards, 7, 10-12, 34,
45, 162
Shorebirds, 28, 51, 124-127
shoreline hardening, 11, 12, 33, 113
shoreline living, 11, 34, 162
Skagit Bay, 9, 18, 81-82, 113
Skagit Island, 109, 115
Skagit River, 25, 85, 93, 132
Smith Prairie Reserve, 135
snails, 20, 66, 98-99, 105
South Whidbey Community
Park, 149
South Whidbey Intermediate
School Trails, 134, 148
South Whidbey State Park, 59,
117, 122, 125, 133, 145
Spartina, 28, 87, 114
Sport Fishing Rules for Washington,
58, 118
Stanwood, 127 (birding)
stewardship, iii, 9-13, 74, 108, 117
Stillaguamish, River, 10, 88, 93, 127
Sunlight Beach Access, 68, 69, 122
surf smelt, see forage fish
swallow, 55, 58, 82, 123

Swan Lake, 33, 52, 124
Swantown Lake, see Swan Lake
Terry's Corner, 15, 160
tidal marsh, see pocket estuary
tides, 1, 2-5, 15, 20, 107
tidelands, public, private, 1-4, 15
tidepools, 13, 87, 114, 123
Tillicum Beach, 93, 115
Triangle Cove, 88, 93, 114
uplands, 2-4, 9, 24, 54
Utsalady, 30, 83-85, 113-114, 115,
126, 160
Vancouver, Captain George, 18,
49, 79
Washington Trout, 93
Washington Vehicle Use Permit, 7,
16, 39, 40, 127, 156
Washington Water Trails
Association, 115
Water Resources Advisory
Committee (WRAC), 12
West Beach Vista, 33, 116
West Penn Cove, 40-41, 109, 116,
122, 124
Whale Museum, The, 116
Whale Sighting Network, 7, 116
whales, 7, 60, 71, 72, 77, 111,
114, 116
Whidbey Institute, 135
Whidbey Watershed Stewards,
73-74
Whidby, Joseph, 18
Windjammer Park, 29, 115, 121,
124, 134, 140
worms, 22, 50, 63, 66, 97-98
zonation, intertidal, 20